# HOW TO LIVE THE CHRISTIAN LIFE

# How to Live the Christian Life

SELWYN HUGHES

KINGSWAY PUBLICATIONS
EASTBOURNE

Original edition first published by Crusade Productions 1974
This edition (revised and extended) first published 1981
Reprinted 1981
Reprinted 1982
Reprinted 1985



ISBN 0 86065 149 5

Except where otherwise indicated, biblical quotations are from the Authorized Version (crown copyright).

TLB = The Living Bible
© Tyndale House Publishers 1971

PHILLIPS = The New Testament in Modern English
by J. B. Phillips © J. B. Phillips 1960

*In the interest of confidentiality, all names and situations have been changed.*

Printed in Great Britain for
KINGSWAY PUBLICATIONS LTD
Lottbridge Drove, Eastbourne, E. Sussex BN23 6NT by
Richard Clay (The Chaucer Press) Ltd, Bungay, Suffolk.
Typesetting by Nuprint Services Ltd, Harpenden, Herts.

TO
the members of
CWR's Worldwide Chain of Prayer
who are praying for a
Holy Spirit revival

# *Contents*

# *Foreword*

For close on two thousand years Jesus Christ has been coming into the lives of men and women and transforming them. Wonderful as our own personal experience of Christ in this day and age might be, we were not the first to feel the impact of his life-changing power.

Some of his earliest disciples were fornicators, drunkards, swindlers, thieves and harlots, but he introduced them to a life that was matchless in its purpose, breathtaking in its potential and limitless in its power. He took the worst of sinners and transformed them into saints, then showed them how to live as befitted the sons and daughters of a heavenly King. He has been doing the same in every century since, and that same life-changing power is available to you and me—today.

There are some who think the Christian lifestyle is one among many. It isn't! It exists in a class all by itself. You do not select it from rivals; it stands alone. Other religions have a framework of ethics or a concept of goodness, but *Christianity is the only religion in the world whose founder came back from the dead to re-live his life within the personalities of his followers.*

After close on thirty years in the Christian ministry I have come to see that the church has spent too much time on belief and not enough on behaviour, as a result of which we have a generation of Christians whose heads are crammed with doctrine but whose feet slip from time to time into ways which are non-Christian and far too similar to a world which they have supposedly renounced.

An examination of the deep potential of the life available in Christ, and how we live it, is therefore the purpose of this book.

SELWYN HUGHES

# 1

# *Designed for Success*

John, a university student, sat in my office gripping his Bible so tightly that his knuckles turned white.

'I don't have to go on like this, do I?' he blurted out desperately.

'Every morning when I get up I say to myself, "Today I am going to try my very hardest to live like a Christian"—but always my best intentions fall apart, and I fall into bed at night utterly exhausted. I feel sometimes I am on the verge of a nervous breakdown.'

Pausing for a moment in which to draw a breath he looked across the room at me with an expression of deep concern and pleaded, 'Tell me, tell me—is this *really* the way to live the Christian life?'

Over the past thirty years in which I have been involved in the area of Christian counselling I have found that far too many believers picture the Christian life as a spiritual struggle in which they strive by a determined act of will to imitate Christ and then reflect him to the world around. Like John the university student, they walk a daily tightrope of fear, desperately trying not to fail, yet finish defeated, discouraged and depressed.

## True Christian living

How then should a Christian live? With *poise,* with *peace* and with *power!* The Christian who really *understands* his relationship to Christ is completely free from strain, secure in the knowledge that God is his heavenly Father and that all things are working towards his ultimate benefit.

The child of God who knows the unique relationship of belonging to the family of God also knows that nothing can work successfully against him, and that God (his Father) would not allow one single happening in his life unless it could be utilized for good. In his mind he knows how to deal with evil thoughts, using them as stepping stones to draw closer to his Lord. When people attempt to make him angry he responds with love, refusing to stoop to the level of 'tit for tat'. Stubbornly resisting the temptation to hold bitterness, he turns every injury into personal motivation and transforms every pain into a pearl.

No jealousy can invade his spirit for no one has anything he wants; he finds everything he needs in Christ. His own special purpose in life is seen by him as unique, and just as God designs every snow flake to be different, he knows too that God has a specific purpose for his life which is different from everyone else in the universe. Joy flows into his life as he pursues this unique purpose and closes in with God's destiny for his life.

Problems are met with praise, for he sees in every one of them a potential benefit. Difficulties are responded to with grace, as he draws from them the lesson that needs to be learned. Trials and temptations are treated like lifelong friends and they become to him the emery stone on which he develops his spirit; the wind of 'misfortune' (to change the metaphor) serves only to give him a greater lift towards the things of God.

In the true Christian life there is no struggle, no striving, no strain. There are battles of course, in which satanic forces are encountered and defeated, but this does not leave him a nervous wreck, for he knows how to let Christ lead the battle and repel the demonic invaders.

A young man, who discovered the secret of letting Christ lead put it this way, 'I heard a noise at the door of my heart, and when I looked through the window I saw Satan and his forces gathering outside. I asked Christ to answer the door, and what do you know—when *he* opened it, there was no one there!'

In an airport on the West Coast of America is a sign that says, 'As you slide down the bannisters of life may all the splinters be pointing the wrong way.' A Christian who knows how to let Christ *live* in his personality is moving with the grain of the universe. He is in fact living life the way God planned it, for Christ is integral to the whole creation (Colossians 1:16, Hebrews 1:3), and as the universe is basically Christian (in the sense that Christ is its centre) then when we live in Christ and he lives in us we are living in harmony with the universe. Life approves of the Christian way because it is written into the texture of God's creation.

In evangelical circles we have emphasized the 'way of salvation' to such an extent that when a person becomes a Christian it seems as if we say, 'Now you're in, turn your attention to friends, relatives, neighbours, and get them to become Christians too.' This is an important project of course, which should be presented to every new Christian, but what is equally important is the concept of living a lifestyle so dynamic and different that others (non-Christians) would gaze at us and say, 'That's the kind of life I would like to live—how can I get it?'

## Failure to reflect Christ

Following an address I gave at a Christian Union meeting in the London area, Tom came up to me and said, 'I believe most of what you said, and there is only one thing hindering me becoming a Christian—why is it that so many Christians are so miserable?' We may as well face it. Those of us who have been Christians for a long time are not very good examples of the faith we profess.

A woman giving out tracts on a street corner tried to press one on a lady passing by. 'Go on, take one' said the Christian, 'it will change your life.' The lady took one look at the grim expression on the face of the woman who was offering the tract and replied, 'No thank you, I have enough troubles already, without taking on any more.'

Too many of us give the impression that when coming to Christ a person will lose rather than gain. I talked with a minister who told me that during a visit to his local doctor he had approached the doctor's receptionist with a view to inviting her to his church. Although it was days later when I saw him he seemed stunned by the reply he had received.

'She told me,' he said, 'that when she saw so many of my members in the surgery on a Monday morning waiting for their weekly supply of sedatives, she really wondered what I had to offer?'

There were tears in his eyes as he looked at me and said, 'Selwyn, it hurt so much because it was true.'

If as Christians we claim to have abundant life, how does it happen that so many of us give so little evidence that this life is superior? We say that God is our Father and is quietly arranging all things to work to our good, yet we fly into a panic at the first approach of trouble. We claim Christ is Lord of our lives, yet when someone tramples on our rights we show by our actions who is really in command. We talk piously about peace, but when tragedy strikes our peace goes into pieces. We preach forgiveness, but let someone injure us and see what happens. The truth is that there is in many of us too great a gap between what we profess and what we are. That gap *must be closed* if we are to offer to the world a true image of the life that is available in Jesus Christ.

Someone has said a person can never understand why he behaves the way he does, nor the importance or implications of his behaviour, until he understands who and what he is. The question of who and what we are must therefore occupy us in these next few paragraphs.

## Made in the image of God

What is man? A dozen different answers could be given to that question, depending on which point of view you take concerning man's real nature and destiny. Some regard him as simply consisting of physical drives alone, and think that he appears on earth for a short span and then vanishes for ever. Others acknowledge some future destiny beyond the grave, but are not quite sure. There are those who claim that man is just a material being of no eternal value, and they say that when man is reduced to his chemical constituents his real worth amounts to no more than a few pounds sterling.

The truth is that in terms of human values man may not be worth much materially, but his real value lies in the fact that he has been made by God and was made in the divine image.

'Then God said, "Let us make a man—someone like ourselves, to be the master of all life upon the earth and in the skies and in the seas." So God made man like his Maker. Like God did God make man; man and maid did he make them. And God blessed them and told them, "Multiply and fill the earth and subdue it; you are masters of the fish and birds and all the animals"' (Genesis 1:26-28 TLB).

When God finished building the universe he looked for something that would act as a top stone to that great achievement—and so he made a man in his own image, to be the crown of his creation. Just what does the Bible mean when it says that man was 'made in the image of God'?

It cannot mean a physical likeness because, as Jesus told the Samaritan woman at the well, 'God is a Spirit: and they that worship him must worship him in spirit and in truth' (John 4:24). It means quite simply that God copied into man the ingredients of personality: these are will, intelligence and emotion.

## The drive within

God is a Person and as such has the ingredients of personality, these being split up as we have already identified in the form of a will, an intelligence and emotion. Sometimes the question is asked, How does God exist? What makes God tick? What drives the Deity? If we look closely into personality we see that the will, intelligence and emotion must have some driving force, some motivating power, have some governing principle.

In God that principle is clearly seen as being *love.* 'He that loveth not knoweth not God; for God is love' (1 John 4:8). God's will, intelligence and emotion are driven and motivated by love. When John said 'God is love' he meant more than God is *loving,* or God is *lovely,* or God *has* love—he meant that the whole of God's personality is driven, motivated and operated by love.

Love is in fact the driving force of the Deity. It splays over into all his activities and attributes. It is the mainspring that moves the heart of God, and is the deep underlying force that governs God's actions in the universe.

And this is how man was made. He was given a personality (will, intelligence and emotion) just like God's and made to operate in the same way, the principal motivation being love. God's image can therefore be seen in man in the sense that God made man like himself to be ruled, governed and fulfilled by the pure quality of love.

In the cool of the day God would come down into the garden of Eden and commune with man, establishing a spiritual communion in which love would flow from God to man, and from man to God. Both Adam and Eve were designed by God to perform properly in response to love, and as long as love motivated their personalities they had unclouded communion with God and fulfilled the purpose for which they were made.

God's design in making man was therefore drawn from his own nature. He made man like himself—a being who could only function properly when motivated by love.

## The great design

We said a little earlier that a person can never understand why he behaves the way he does, nor the importance or implications of his behaviour, until he understands who and what he is. Our needs as human beings can never be fully realized until we are rightly related to God. We have a design within us that revolves around a centre which is love-related, and that love is not a selfish human love but a love that flows into us from God himself.

Life was made to orbit around the central force of God's meaning for our lives, and anyone who tries to order their lives around any other pivotal point will become bored, restless, frustrated and unfulfilled. He is not functioning as God designed.

If a person behaves like an animal you can be sure he does not know *who he is.* Made in the image of God with a personality that responds properly to love, no man can know a meaningful existence on this earth until God rules at the centre of his life.

## Satan attacks the first human pair

God set the first human pair in a beautiful garden and gave them perfect liberty to enjoy the fruit of every tree in the garden, with the exception of one—the tree of knowledge of good and evil. It was in this garden that the first human sin took place, and the biblical account of this is a model of the problem that we face right here in the twentieth century.

> The serpent was the craftiest of all the creatures the Lord God had made. So the serpent came to the woman. 'Really?' he asked. '*None* of the fruit in the garden? God says you mustn't eat *any* of it?'
>
> 'Of course we may eat it,' the woman told him. 'It's only the fruit from the tree at the *centre* of the garden that we are not to eat. God says we mustn't eat it or even touch it, or we will die.' 'That's a lie!' the serpent hissed. 'You'll not die! God knows very well that the instant you eat it you will become like him, for your eyes will be opened—you will be able to distinguish good from evil! [Genesis 3:1-5 TLB.]

The appeal of Satan in his first encounter with the woman whom God had made was based on her self-interest. When faced with this temptation from the Adversary she began to wonder whether she was missing out on something, and the longer she pondered this the more it created doubt in her mind that God really was good, and encouraged her to seek for things which God disallowed. Once she took of that forbidden fruit and violated God's instructions she immediately pushed God from the centre of her life and placed her own self-interest in *his* place.

This is in fact what sin is all about. It is choosing our own way rather than God's way, and it was not long after Eve's violation of God's command that Adam took the same step, thereby separating himself from the pivotal centre of God's love and goodness around which he had been designed to revolve.

## Man's basic sin is egocentricity

People often regard sin as the performance of evil actions, such as murder, adultery, fornication, but these are simply the outward evidences of an inner disharmony. Man's basic problem is that he has dislodged God from the centre of his being and has in turn set up self-interest, egocentricity and self-worship in place of the Almighty.

Immediately Adam and Eve did this God was obliged to separate himself from the erring pair, and the love of God (their inner motivation) supplying the power to their personalities was instantly cut off. But as personality cannot exist without some governing principle Adam and Eve were then obliged to provide another motivation as a driving force for their own existence and that motivation proved to be self-interest, or selfishness, or if you prefer—egocentricity.

This then is the condition into which man has fallen. Designed by God with a personality that only operates properly when fed by his love, man has now separated himself from that stream of eternal love and seeks to run his life on another motivation which is basically egocentric and full of self-interest. In the centre of his life he has set up a governing principle which is built around himself. The big 'I' dominates the scene, and he has positioned himself in the centre of his universe bending everything to his own desires and catering for his own self-interest.

Sin has to be seen as refusing God his rightful place in the centre of our beings. If we regard sin simply as acts of sensuality, or works of wickedness, we fail to distinguish between the effect and the cause. Sin is saying to God, 'I want to run my own life. I don't want you telling me what to do, nor anyone else for that matter. I am the captain of my ship. I am the master of my soul.'

It is in fact a refusal on man's part to honour God as God. It may not even be a denial of God's existence, nor even a rejection of the philosophical concept of God, for we can believe in God, worship God, and still not know him, for until we replace God at the centre of our existence there can be no real purpose or meaning to life.

It is only as we deal firmly with this deep problem of egocentricity that we can move forward to live according to the design God has for our lives. Fulfilment comes in our functioning the way God designed us.

# 2

# *A Joyful Exchange*

David, a shy young engineering student, would only agree to attend a counselling session if his wife was allowed to be present. In fact she had to become his spokesman at each session, but it was not long before the basic problem was uncovered when she identified his problem in these words.

'David doesn't *feel* saved. He went forward at a large evangelistic rally and was counselled by someone who told him how to receive Christ, but he seems to lack the assurance that he is a true Christian. What steps does he need to take to remove these doubts, and know for sure that he is really saved?'

It took just forty-five minutes to deal with this problem and David left the counselling room with a shine upon his face that his wife said she had never seen before. When I met them in a church months later he still radiated that genuine sense of assurance and with a smile he told me that, since that day some months before, he had added a new degree to his list of credits. Knowing something of his engineering studies I was puzzled when he said that he had an M.A. degree.

'M.A.,' I said '—I didn't know you were studying for that!'

'I didn't study for it,' he added, 'God gave it to me that day in your office. It means Mightily Assured.'

Some of the steps I took David through I want to share with you now.

## True Conversion

The initial act of moving self from the throne of our beings and allowing God to come in at the centre of our whole existence is called in the Bible 'conversion'. Our basic sin of egocentricity is so ingrained that no human process will ever correct it, and there is no therapy in the world that can dethrone self and enthrone Christ apart from that dramatic experience know as 'conversion' or, as it is sometimes termed, 'the new birth.'

The Old Testament recognized this in such statements as these. 'I will give them hearts that respond to me. They shall be my people and I will be their God . . . . The day will come, says the Lord, when I will make a new contract with the people of Israel . . . . I will inscribe my laws upon their hearts, so that they shall *want* to honour me' (Jeremiah 24:7; 31:31-33 TLB, italics mine).

Jesus said to Nicodemus, a religious ruler in Jerusalem, 'With all the earnestness I possess I tell you this: Unless you are born again, you can never get into the Kingdom of God' (John 3:3 TLB).

We have seen that egocentricity is responsible for keeping self at the centre of our beings, and the manner in which this is dealt with at conversion is so important that unless it is clearly understood and accepted it can result in continued conflicts within the soul. David's problem stemmed from the fact that at the time of his commitment to Christ he had never really allowed Christ to occupy the centre of his life, but simply relegated him to a position *close to the centre,* which of course is not true conversion, and can only result in uncertainty and lack of assurance. We must now clarify the whole meaning of conversion to see the importance of that first step into Christian experience and understand how, when done properly, it points life in the direction God has determined.

## Evil of pride

The innate desire to keep self at the centre of our beings is defined in the Bible as pride. Pride is the *deadliest* of the seven deadly sins! The theologians were right when they classified it as the most venomous disease of the soul. There are some however who feel that it is not as bad as lust, cruelty or even greed, but when one understands what pride really is it stands out as the foulest and most evil of all our enemies.

Pride builds barriers between men and God, and between the strata of human society. It keeps apart the races and encourages a sense of superiority in one nation over another. But its worst evil is this—*it robs God of his rightful place at the centre of our lives.* It has been described by someone as the 'Devil's finished handiwork' and led the great William Law to say, 'Pride must die in you or Christ cannot live in you.'

It is impossible to see ourselves as we really are when pride takes up a position of strength within our being. It takes issue with the plain statements of God's word which claim that 'all have sinned, and come short of the glory of God' (Romans 3:23) and tends to explain away sin as simply the 'growing pains of the human race' or 'darkness where the light should be'.

Pride is a refusal to honour God as God and fails to see that his rightful place is at the centre of our existence. And this rejection of God as the spiritual centre of our being is the basic factor behind all evil. How can we go about dethroning pride and enthroning God in his rightful place within our beings? What steps can we take to beat down this evil until God takes full and complete control?

It begins with a *meaningful commitment* to Christ, and continues as he is allowed to rule in our lives and is accepted as our rightful Lord. Pride is dislodged to a major degree when Christ is admitted into our lives at conversion. The Christian life in fact begins with a crushing defeat to pride as Christ is recognized as the rightful owner of our lives. Let's bring the facts a little more closely into focus as we attempt to see what really happens when Christ comes in and sets up his throne within a human heart.

## What is a Christian?

The Christian life begins when by personal invitation we allow Christ to enter into our lives. Some think that to be a Christian one has simply to be born in a Christian country, while others feel that providing they can keep out of the hands of the police and make some effort to live a reasonably good life they lay an honest claim to the term. There are those also who would argue that the rite of 'infant baptism' entitles them to being called 'Christians', although many in their more honest moments would admit that like some cases of vaccination, it just didn't 'take'. To those who claim that attending church gives them the right to be called Christians, Billy Graham has a classic reply: 'Going to church does not automatically make a man a Christian any more than going to a garage makes him a motor car.'

According to the New Testament a Christian is a person in whom Christ *lives.* We are indebted to Paul perhaps more than any other New Testament writer for a clear definition of the term 'Christian', and he presents it from two entirely different points of view. First, he points out that a Christian is a person who has been made anew in Christ. 'If any man be in Christ, he is a new creature' (2

Corinthians 5:17). The phrase 'in Christ' occurs over and over again in Paul's writings, and someone who has counted the frequency of the expression (or similar terms such as 'in him') claims that it occurs no fewer than 164 times. Paul never ceased to marvel at the wonder of being made anew in his Lord.

Many Christians can of course remember the day (and even the hour) when Christ came into their lives, but there are others who although they cannot identify a moment or period of conversion know without any shadow of doubt that he lives in their lives. For them conversion wasn't a blinding flash but a gradual dawning of a new day in which they learned to trust Christ and recognize his presence deep within their lives. Such people should not be troubled by their inability to point to a moment of conversion, providing of course they are fully aware of Christ's presence in their hearts and his complete lordship over their lives. After all the best evidence of our being alive is not our birth certificate but rather the fact that blood flows through our veins and life pulses through our beings.

Sometimes, however, there are those who say, 'I can remember committing my life to Jesus Christ but for some reason I do not *feel* saved,' or, 'I have prayed and asked the Lord to receive me but I have no assurance of salvation.' In such situations where people lack definite assurance, it is normally due to the fact that at the time of their encounter with Christ they did not make a meaningful commitment in which their whole being was involved.

## A joyful exchange

A meaningful relationship with Christ begins with surrender, and surrender is what Luther called 'a joyful exchange'. It's a swap—your life for his and his life for yours. The more of yourself you give to him the more of himself he will give to you.

Psychology tells us that the aim of every individual life is maturity. Achieving maturity involves dislodging our egocentricity so that the actual centre of our being can be established and become the full motivation of our lives. How, you ask, can we dislodge egocentricity? Or in other words, how can we get ourselves off our hands? The best way is to put yourself in God's hands, and the more clearly this is understood at the moment of surrender the less likely will problems occur at a later stage of Christian experience. I am convinced that many serious problems which emerge in some Christians' lives stem from a lack of clear understanding as to what should happen when Christ comes in and takes up his abode in a human heart.

Christ must be admitted into our lives as *Lord.* If he is received, then it is to be on his terms and not ours. This means of course that some things will have to go, sin being the first, and no commitment to Christ can be complete until the question of past sin is dealt with in its entirety. Everyone has some sin in his life, but because of Christ's sacrifice and death on Calvary God has made it clear that he is ready to forgive and blot out every sin when we turn to him for forgiveness and call upon him for pardon.

The Bible has a very special word to describe this act of turning from sin; it is called *repentance.* It means more than being sorry for sin. Someone described it 'being sorry enough to quit'. Repentance is agreeing with God about our sin and being ready to hand it over to him for cleansing, forgiveness, pardon and release.

The way in which we repent of sin is extremely important. Some on the threshold of commitment to Christ simply see their sin as something which has got them into a deal of trouble and are merely sorry for the consequences. Repentance is not being sorry for the *consequences* of sin, but being sorry over the *sin itself.* A failure to understand this is responsible for the lack of assurance in the hearts and lives of many of Christ's followers. Incomplete repentance gives rise to feelings of insecurity, as the heart is not visited by divine forgiveness and pardon.

## Incomplete repentance causes lack of assurance

Sometimes a person will be prepared to repent of every sin except one, knowing that if this particular sin is revealed it may involve them in restitution or consequent court action. Real repentance (the only way to a positive assurance of divine pardon and forgiveness) involves making right any offences which may have been committed.

If when you become a Christian you struggled over the 'will I have to give up ---?' (naming a particular sin or habit) then you were obviously having a deep struggle as to who should have central place in your life! If God is to come into our lives, then he must be given his rightful place at the centre of our whole existence. Someone has likened sin to *anarchy.* Crime is breaking the laws of a nation, but anarchy challenges the right of the nation to make such laws. 'Sin,' said Wesley Nelson in *Captivated by Christ,* 'is more than breaking God's commandments; it challenges the very right of God to rule.'

Complete repentance is turning from every sin and recognizing that the most evil thing about it is not so much that it breaks God's commandments, but that it breaks his heart. Among the Syrian Christians of South India is a centuries-old custom in which the first words spoken to a new-born child are 'Jesus Christ is Lord'. In the same way, when a person becomes a Christian the same words are addressed to him by the Holy Spirit (1 Corinthians 12:3).

Christ *must* come in as Lord.

His lordship must extend over *every* area of our lives.

Right down through the centuries there have been those who have invited Christ to come into their lives but have sought to uphold their own authority in certain areas of their beings. Lordship means that his rule extends over every area of our lives, and Christ's insistence on this has deep strategy.

If he is to keep us free from evil then he must have the territory of our lives completely in his hands. Temptation seeks always to find some foothold in our lives on which it can fasten itself, then once this is accomplished it goes on to establish a bridge-head over which it sends its sappers to fortify the position and take over control. Christ makes it clear from the beginning that he cannot consent to being excluded from territory which the enemy could use to undermine his authority or weaken his control.

## Christ only fits in at the centre

In the New Testament we read of a rich young ruler who wanted to be a follower of Christ but was not willing to move his riches out of the centre of his life so that Christ could take over control. The apostle Paul on the other hand made a complete commitment to Christ in which he invited the Master into the centre of his being. 'Lord, what wilt thou have me to do?' (Acts 9:6). It is only as we accept Christ into the centre of our existence that we enjoy the deep assurance that comes through knowing that he lives in our lives as *Lord* and that every area of our being is under his complete control.

'If we do not crown him Lord of all, we do not crown him Lord at all.'

Our Saviour's lordship must be for *life.* A famous preacher of this present century, Dr. W.E. Sangster, has pointed out that when Christ comes into a person's life he comes in, not as a president but as a king. 'A president,' says Sangster, 'serves for a period and goes out of office. A king rules for life.'

Christ's lordship must not only extend over every area of our lives, but it must stretch through the *whole* of our lives. The vows of personal commitment to Christ must be for life; they cover not only time *but eternity too.* A wife does not say to her husband at frequent intervals 'let's get married all over again' for she knows that the vows she took at the moment of marriage were for the whole of her life. It is the same with our relationship to Christ—we are his now, and for the rest of our days. And eternity too!

There is no way to sure enjoyment of the Christian life that leaves out the complete lordship of Jesus Christ. Augustine said in his *Confessions* some fifteen hundred years ago, 'Thou hast made us for thyself, and our heart is restless till it finds its rest in thee.'

# 3

# *Understanding Your Self-image*

Mr and Mrs Davies brought their sixteen-year-old son Roger for counselling because, as they put it, 'we can't cure him of lying, exaggeration, and rebellion.' After listening to a general discussion in which all three members of the family participated I decided to talk with each person individually and set up three different counselling sessions accordingly.

I took Roger's father first, and in his session he told me how he had fought against so many difficulties in his life, having been taken out of school at an early age to work in his father's failing business. At the age of seventeen his father died, leaving him responsible for the family, but with hard work and determination he had built the business to what it was today, a thriving and going concern.

Mrs Davies told me of her constant arguments with Roger and how so often she would burst into tears when confronted by his attitude of rebellion. She in fact shed several tears during the whole course of our session together.

It was Roger himself, however, who provided me with the key to the whole situation. In answer to my probings he admitted that his father often made comparisons, indicating how hard he had worked when he was a child and stating that Roger needed to 'pull himself together because he would never be any good'. His mother, too, joined in this personal abuse, and more than once burst into tears in front of him saying, 'Don't you realize what you are doing to your father and me?'

Roger had now grown into a boy who was extremely rebellious, insecure, fearful and sullen. Although he had made a commitment to Christ he still felt deeply rejected at home, and shared some of his deepest and intimate feelings with me. Although there were many surface problems showing themselves in Roger's life, as we talked it became obvious that his basic problem was self-rejection.

I shared some insights with him and, although all his problems were not solved in that interview, the change that came over him was remarkable. His parents told me months later that he had taken on the job of evangelistic secretary in the local church and was busy directing one outreach after another. Their home, they said, was now so different since Roger had changed.

Unfortunately my advice to them personally had carried little weight, but I was glad that Roger had taken the steps necessary to accept himself and see his real worth and value first as an individual, and then as a corporate member of the church of Jesus Christ.

## Humility and inferiority

In the previous chapter we saw how pride received a major defeat when Christ came in at conversion, but we need to look a little deeper into the problem and examine the very subtle difference between humility (the opposite of pride) and inferiority.

There are many Christians who, recognizing that pride is an evil force that has to be firmly dealt with in their lives, fail to see the difference between humility and inferiority, and are caught up in a self-hatred which is entirely unsupported by the Scriptures. If pride is sin, they argue, then we must despise ourselves and not allow any feeling of self-worth to remain within our beings.

Fifty years ago the term 'inferiority complex' was hardly known, except to psychologists, psychiatrists, doctors and social workers, but now it is in common use, and is understood (to some degree at least) by almost everyone. Dr Adler first gave the word currency but complained in later years that it had been misused and given a twist which he had never intended in his original definition of the term.

An inferiority complex normally develops in childhood and unless corrected can damage the potential of a person's life, bringing them to the edge of self-hatred and self-rejection. In a Christian it is something that must be carefully watched and corrected, as it can lead to a false sense of humility in which we imagine ourselves to be humble only to find we are really living out the consequences of an inferiority complex and a negative self-image.

It occurs (as we have said) in early life, during the formative years of our existence. A young child has no clear picture of himself and sees himself in the mirror of his abilities, his appearance and his character. A child's sense of values is based upon what any authority figure—such as a parent, or a schoolteacher—tells him, and the ideas he gains from such people help to construct his self-image. This is enlarged somewhat by the values that other people place on his appearance or abilities and by the statements that are made concerning these two things. Often times while growing up, children, with that unthinking cruelty which is so characteristic, will ask, 'Why is your nose crooked?' or 'Did you know that your ears stick out?' or

'What size shoes do you *really* wear?'

In a counselling session Beryl explained that during her childhood her father never gave her any praise and she was told over and over again, 'You will never be any good.' As a small child she had no alternative but to accept the verdict of her father, and years later it developed into a serious conflict which took several hours of in-depth counselling to correct.

While inferiority shows itself mainly in feelings of self-rejection, it can display itself in another form too. Dr Alder was quick to point out when he first introduced the term 'inferiority complex' that it can sometimes assume the manner of superiority and mislead many into thinking it is a different problem. In such cases it is but a disguise of the self-hate about which we have been talking, and is really a supreme effort of the will to move oneself out of the rut into which one has fallen.

We can easily see why some regard the secret self-despising of oneself as humility, but basically it is as much pride as the braggart, swaggering attitude that struts around saying, 'Look at me—see what a wonderful person I really am.' If self-rejection is an inverted form of pride, how can we begin to sweep it clean out of our soul and live out our lives free from its evil grasp?

## A positive self-image

Jesus gave us the answer in his interview recorded for us in the first chapter of John's Gospel. 'And when Jesus beheld him, he said, Thou art Simon the son of Jona: thou shalt be called Cephas, which is by interpretation, A stone' (John 1:42) In the Greek text there are subtle shades of difference in the words 'Simon' and 'a stone'. The truth is best brought out in a translation which reads 'Thou art Simon (a reed) but thou shalt be Cephas (a stone).'

Jesus presented to the erring Simon Peter a completely new image of himself. As men looked at Peter they saw instability and change, but as Christ looked at him he could see hidden depths that others could not plumb and he knew that by his love and power he could make Peter the man he should be. He was saying in effect, 'Peter, men see in you instability and change. You are only too aware of this yourself. But I can change you. My love and my power can work in you towards a complete transformation of your life. I see you not as you are but as you can be when you respond fully to my love.'

In discovering a proper self-image we must learn to see ourselves as 'in Christ'. There are some who teach that a full and meaningful life arises from self-realization, in which we learn to draw upon the powers deep within us and thereby extend our personalities and enlarge our beings. In a special course I conducted on the subject of 'Life in a New Dimension' a small group of university students enrolled thinking it was a course on self-realization, but half-way through they came to me and expressed their desire to surrender to Jesus Christ. What had happened? They came to see that life only works properly when God is at the centre, and as they surrendered they discovered the secret that success in life stems not from self-realization, but Christ-realization.

When Christ confronted Peter with those dramatic words in John 1:42, 'You are a reed—you shall be a rock,' he was attempting to show him that life can only be fully realized when the whole being is surrendered to the transforming power of the lordship of Christ.

What then are the principles of self-acceptance? How can we begin to overcome inferiority and build up a positive self-image in which we see ourselves complete 'in Christ'?

## The highest value

One of the deepest needs within our beings is the need we have to feel of value and of real worth, and to realize this of course we need to live consistently a life in which we, and others, recognize this value.

The Bible has sometimes been criticized as contributing to man's poor self-image because of the doctrine of man's total depravity, but the Bible is only being honest about man's plight and condition. Man's guilt in the Scriptures is never presented in order to lead him to despair, but to deliverance. It is true that all men have sinned and come short of the glory of God, but this is only one part of the story. God in Christ has paid the penalty for human sin, and when man accepts the forgiveness, healing and cleansing offered him, he then (and only then) has the chance of functioning as God designed him.

That design in man's being included the principle of obedience, and no one can feel of proper value to God until he has confessed his basic sin (egocentricity and pride) and obediently turns himself over to the complete lordship of Christ, hour by hour, and day by day. When we do this we then function as children of God, as members of his family; this is what he intended for us from the beginning of creation.

When we look into the Scriptures and see the tremendous value God places upon our lives we cannot help being staggered by some of the statements we find in the book of God. Jesus taught his disciples that they were of immense value to their heavenly Father. He said, 'What is the price of five sparrows? A couple of pennies? Not much more than that. Yet God does not forget a single one of them. And he knows the number of hairs on your head! Never fear, you are far more valuable to him than a whole flock of sparrows' (Luke 12:6-7 TLB).

Paul in his epistle to the Ephesians prayed earnestly that those who knew Christ would also come to understand their own value in the sight of God. He writes, 'I want you to realize that God has been made *rich* because we who are Christ's have been given to him!' (TLB italics mine). There must be thousands of believers who cannot accept the idea that God is enriched by having *them*, but nevertheless it is absolutely true.

We can usually judge the value of anything by the price that a qualified person places upon an object, and by that criterion man is the most valuable part of God's creation, for he allowed his only begotten Son to die for him. No man is to be despised (even by himself) when the eternal God was willing to die for him!

## God's investment in us

Having been given the central place in our beings at conversion Christ then proceeds, *with our consent and co-operation,* to develop his specific purpose for our lives. This, one of the most powerful truths in the whole universe, is presented by Matthew Henry in the following way.

'Consider the fact that you are "custom made" by God. Your genes, chromosomes, and all factors contributing to your being were governed by your Creator. All of this was done because you were designed to fulfil a specific purpose in history—a purpose no one else can completely fulfil. The fulfilment of this ultimate purpose is left within your power. It depends on the way *you respond to your Creator.*'

God has a special and specific purpose for every life he indwells, and the discovery of this purpose is the greatest influencing factor to the development of a positive self-image. This principle can be seen at work in the life of

Jesus Christ. It was said of him that 'he finished the work his Father gave him to do'. Having discovered the specific ministry and function God had planned for his life Jesus Christ closed in with it and completed it to the glory of God his Father.

Just as God had a specific purpose for his Son so he has a special purpose for your life too! That purpose is unique inasmuch as no other human being in the universe can properly convey the message that God has designed to be revealed to the world through you. Once we realize that God has a unique design for our lives, and that we are not just machines on an assembly line, an exciting new concept of living opens up to us.

Just think of it! There is no one else in this universe *exactly* like you! Just as no two snow flakes are identically the same, nor two blades of grass exactly alike, so no two human beings are identical to each other psychologically, physically or spiritually. If God has gone to the trouble of making sure that no two snow flakes carry an identical message, or no two blades of grass duplicate each other, then how much more does he want that same design, wisdom and power to be displayed in the men and women who reflect his own divine image.

## Happiness through self-acceptance

Some Christians find it hard to give themselves entirely to God because of dissatisfaction with their own self-image. Thousands of Christians complain continually about their physical, psychological and spiritual make-up.

'If only I were taller,' says one. 'If only I were shorter,' says another. 'I wish my eyes were blue instead of brown,' complains a young girl looking into the mirror. Our failure to accept ourselves as God has designed us can lead in turn to a rejection of self, hindering the development of

God's purpose for our lives.

If we reject the unchangeable features of our being such as our height, skin colour, eyes, etc, we can unconsciously build up a floating bitterness against God which lies deep beneath our conscious minds yet reasons thus: 'God—if I had been in your place when you made me I would have made a far better job of me that you did.' The hidden resentment sometimes surfaces in a lack of trust, for how can you trust a Creator who slipped up on such an important matter as your physical appearance?

Why, says someone, should even a trivial thing like this be discussed? If I am not satisfied with my appearance surely this will not hinder me from pursuing God's purpose for my life? Quite simply we must see that self-honesty is essential to honesty with God. If we cannot accept ourselves as God has made us then the problems this creates will surface in our work, our prayer time, our witness, our worship and our service for God.

Ralph came for counselling several times complaining that he was unable to trust God, was always exaggerating, and tended to push himself to the front in conversations, prayer meetings and at his place of work. He was asked a simple question which sometimes counsellors use when seeking to test a person's self-rejection.

'If you had the power to change anything about you, how would you use it?'

'I think,' he said, 'I would use it to change my height.'

Further counselling brought out the deep bitterness that Ralph had towards life due to the fact that he wished he was taller. He saw how this self-rejection caused his distrust of God, and how it impelled him to compensate for what he thought was an inferior self-image by continually pushing himself to the forefront of conversations and turning all situations to centre upon himself.

Jean, a fine young girl from a Christian family, came to

me for counselling, but as I was busy I arranged for an associate to take the interview. Jean's problem it seemed was over-attention to dress, and an over-concern for her whole appearance. She would spend hours before the mirror changing her hair style continually, but was never satisfied with the end result. Her counsellor noticed a tendency to name-drop and self-centred conversation in which she was either self-exalting or self-condemning.

Gradually through a few hours of counselling she was brought to see that the problems which concerned her were just the symptoms of deeper inner conflicts stemming from a frustrated desire to be like someone else. In a simple prayer she accepted herself as a unique creation of God, submitted herself entirely into God's hands, praised him for the specific achievement he had planned for her, then closed in with God's plan for her life. The symptoms disappeared overnight. Self-acceptance set her on the road to a new identity with Christ.

From the moment of conversion Christ is in us working to eliminate that arrogant, thrustful, demanding and dominating self, and to give us a true understanding of our proper worth.

A Christian's dignity arises from an understanding of his relationship to Christ. How can a child of a king feel inferior? How can a blood-bought sinner feel proud? To accept ourselves as a unique creation from the hand of God, and to recognize that we are designed for specific achievement, will enable us to put down inferiority and to stand in all humility with praise and adoration to a Father whose eternal designs are beyond our understanding.

# 4

# 'Out of Seven into Eight'

Carol could hardly wait to be seated in my office before she tearfully blurted out, 'I can't understand it. Life has been so wonderful since I gave my heart to Christ... but now I feel such a failure. I don't think I can go on any more.'

Carol had been a Christian for just over three months. In fact she had come forward during a Sunday night evangelistic service in a church I was then pastoring, so I knew something of her conversion and subsequent Christian experience.

From the first moment of her conversion Carol had radiated a joy which was infectious. Everyone loved to be in her company and I regarded her Christian witness and testimony as one of the most impressive I had ever seen. What had happened to reduce this pretty seventeen-year-old girl to the verge of despair?

'After I became a Christian,' she went on, 'I thought all my troubles would be over... and for six weeks everything was fine... but now I have so many problems which even though I pray about never seem to go away. I have wrong thoughts, bad desires and other things which keep rising up within me, and I don't seem to be able to do anything about them. Isn't there some way I can be free from this terrible conflict within me?'

Carol was discovering early in her Christian experience that despite her radical conversion there were still carnal tendencies within her. She had thought that at conversion all these things were uprooted and she would never have to face them again, but now with the realization that carnality was still present (to some degree at least) she became utterly confused and dispirited. Although she didn't realize it, she was in fact echoing the words of the apostle Paul who described the self-same conflict in the following dramatic words—twenty centuries before Carol had been born:

> My own behaviour baffles me. For I find myself not doing what I really want to do but doing what I really loathe. Yet surely if I do things that I really don't want to do, I am admitting that I really agree with the Law... I often find that I have the will to do good, but not the power.... When I come up against the Law I want to do good, but in practice I do evil.... In my mind I am God's willing servant, but in my own nature I am bound fast, as I say, to the law of sin and death. It is an agonising situation, and who on earth can set me free from the clutches of my own sinful nature? I thank God there is a way out through Jesus Christ our Lord.
> [Romans 7:15-16, 18, 21-25 PHILLIPS.]

## The inward conflict

According to the apostle Paul there are within every Christian two powerful forces at work. One seeks to drag us downward; the other seeks to lift us upward. This dichotomy or inward struggle can only be resolved when we allow Christ to reach deep into our lives and free us from the bondage which sin brings.

In most cases of conversion a person experiences a remarkable sense of freedom and inward release which affects different people in different ways. The consequences of Christ's entry into human life is for some so staggering they consider this new found experience to be a constant 'high' from which they will never descend. Under the inspiration of this new happiness they meet all their problems 'head on' and regard each day as a continual 'joyride with Jesus'. Gradually, however, the new Christian begins to adjust to this new lifestyle and realizes he is still a creature of flesh; for some this moment of self-revelation can be a depressing and disturbing disclosure.

This in fact was part of Carol's problem who, becoming acutely aware of the lower nature still active within her, displayed feelings of depression and despair which in turn caused her to wonder whether or not she had experienced a true conversion. The evil hints of jealousy, the subtle rising of lust, the upward surge of carnal desires, conspired to produce a sense of despair which has been shared by many Christians throughout the whole of the Christian era.

Of course before conversion these things did not trouble her too much, but at her conversion the Spirit of God united with her spirit, strengthening her conscience and producing within her a deep desire for a transformed life. Her thoughts, however, continued to manifest conflicting desires, and whether she liked it or not she was caught up in an inner conflict shared by all who make a meaningful commitment to Christ. I explained to her that as she comprehended with her spirit the image of Christ she would become more and more dissatisfied with her present deficiences and would long for a more complete image based on a true likeness to the Lord Jesus Christ.

When Carol saw this insight into what was going on deep within her personality she began to look a little more like the girl I had always known. We went on of course (as we shall do now) to discuss the problem more deeply, but it was not long before Carol left me with the same radiancy I saw the night she committed her life to Jesus Christ.

## A new standard of comparison

Following conversion a Christian has a standard of comparison which he had never had before—the Person of Christ resident within his life. It is only as we look at Christ that we see ourselves as we really are. Nobody really sees himself as he really is until he sees himself in Christ. He and he alone reflects a perfect likeness of the image which falls upon him. When a man looks into the mirror of the Person of Christ he can say with all truth, 'That is the person I am.'

Our aim then should be constantly to contrast and compare the persons we are to the Person he is; to take a mirror as it were of Christ's life revealed to us in the gospels and to see ourselves in him. Our Lord drew a very clear picture of the way life should be lived in those famous words recorded for us in what is popularly termed 'the Beatitudes', or as Billy Graham calls them, 'the Beautiful Attitudes' (Matthew 5:3-12). The eight qualities of the 'Sermon on the Mount', as it is otherwise called, contains the key to successful Christian living. Christ first exemplified these qualities in his own life, then laid them down as the standard for all his followers.

Obeying these principles we move forward to success; violating them we are dragged down into serious conflicts. 'Be ye therefore perfect,' said Jesus, 'even as your Father ... in heaven is perfect' (Matthew 5:48). If you think he raises the standard to unbelievable heights remember he also imparts the power to achieve it. He not only carries the moral test into the deepest recesses of the soul but makes his grace freely available, by which we can pass it.

The only place where a person can see the truth about himself is in Christ. Our enemies of course will tell us what they *think* about us but they so often speak in anger that they tend to exaggerate our faults and minimize our virtues. Those who love us on the other hand tend to overlook our failings and even if they see them they would rather put up with them than hurt us by bringing them to our attention. Only Christ can reveal our lives. We see ourselves *clearly* in him.

## Facing the truth

Some Christians find this penetrating diagnosis of their inner life to be more than they can face and tend to go through the most fantastic mental gymnastics to hide from the truth. This can be one of the most challenging moments of the whole Christian experience as one comes under the revealing reflection of Christ, and any attempt to conceal the truth about oneself can result in even deeper problems.

It is not flattering to the human heart to discover this inbred egocentricity, and the experience of spiritual rebirth serves only to drive into greater prominence the evil that resides within. It is important to realize here that the presence of evil thoughts or desire is not in itself sin. Life comes to us with powerful instinctive urges and as Christians God instructs us not to weakly yield ourselves to the varying stresses of instinct but to build a life in which morals shall regulate our appetites and spiritual purpose guide the passions of the flesh.

Temptation is not sin. An evil or sensual thought can rise unbidden to the mind prompted by a word, a picture, a story, an advertisement or even an odour—but that in itself is not sin. It becomes sin when the self welcomes it, adopts it, owns it and nurtures it. It does not need in some cases to solidify in an act to become sin, but the fondling of the thought and concentration upon it can be as much sin as the act itself. Jesus said that if a man identifies with the lust that rises up within him and harbours the thought, allowing it to monopolize his mind, he is as guilty as if he actually committed the *act* of adultery.

Admittedly it is painful to expose ourselves to the soul-searching light of Christ and his word, and some are so adept at repressing and denying the fact of inbred sin that they become quite unaware that it exists. Denial of the problem does nothing to solve it, and it is only as we face these things that we can take the necessary steps to release and inner harmony.

Is it not ironic that when a person first becomes a Christian he honestly opens himself up to Jesus Christ, confessing his sin, but as he progresses in his Christian experience he sometimes tries to cover up his problems and pretend they don't exist? It is this repression and 'mask wearing' that Dr William Miller, a Christian psychiatrist, claims is one of the major causes of emotional breakdowns. We must see that at conversion we are saved from the *penalty* of our sins, but we continually need to rely upon that same grace of God to save us daily from the *power* of sin.

## The carnal nature

At this stage someone might ask 'What really is the carnal nature? How does it work within me? Is there any way it can be overcome?'

The Bible uses several terms to identify the carnal nature. It refers to it sometimes as the 'flesh' (Greek, *sarx*) 'the old man' or 'sinful nature'. The apostle Paul, without doubt the greatest exponent on this subject, explains it this way: 'For the flesh lusteth against the

Spirit, and the Spirit against the flesh: and these are contrary the one to the other: so that ye cannot do the things that ye would' (Galatians 5:17).

A careful study of the scriptures relating to the subject of the 'carnal nature' will reveal two basic facts:

1. It is the basic nature which we have when we are born, which is at enmity with God being self-centred, egocentric and rebellious (Romans 7:14-24; 8:5-8).

2. It cannot be completely eradicated until we receive our transformed resurrection bodies, but its power to operate in the life of a Christian is neutralized when we learn to submit to the complete lordship of Jesus Christ (Romans 7:25; 1 John 1:8-10).

We saw in a previous chapter that man's basic sin is egocentricity. He is set on an ego trip from which he does not wish to change course, and looks at everything with an eye as to how it will affect *him*. Egocentricity will always seek to magnify itself. It is touchy, sensitive when not recognized, and struggles for the highest position of honour and praise. It cannot bear to be rebuked or corrected; it is full of defence. It is destructive, disturbing and deadly. In his epistle to the Galatians Paul gives us a list of things which arise from this inbred sinfulness: 'The activities of the lower nature are obvious ... sexual immorality, impurity of mind, sensuality, worship of false gods, witchcraft, hatred, quarrelling, jealousy, bad temper, rivalry, factions, party-spirit, envy, drunkenness, orgies and things like that' (Galatians 5:19-21 PHILLIPS).

How then do we deal with this indwelling force that is basic to our nature? How can we be set free?

## The way out

When the apostle Paul asked, 'Who on earth can set me free from the clutches of my own sinful nature?' he went on to answer his own question in this way: 'I thank God there is a way out through Jesus Christ our Lord' (Romans 7:24-25 PHILLIPS). The chapter that follows this is one of the greatest chapters in the Bible, for there Paul marshals the facts and the principles which enabled him to overcome the downward pull of the carnal nature and rise in the power of the Spirit to a life of constant victory. He passes from the gloom of Romans 7 into the sunshine of Romans 8. Out of 7 and into 8, as it were, should be the experience of every believer, for God does not wish us to live under bondage to sin, but to enjoy the provision he has made through his Son, the Lord Jesus Christ, and the dynamic Person of the Holy Spirit.

Those who have discovered the principles which enable them to live above the bondage of the lower nature use an expressive word to describe it—*free!* Paul put it this way: 'For the law of the Spirit of life in Christ Jesus hath *made me free* from the law of sin and death' (Romans 8:2). 'Spiritual freedom' writes a contemporary, 'is not the right to do what we want, but the power to do what we ought.' Paul adds this further word, 'It is to *freedom* that you have been called, my brothers. Only be careful that freedom does not become mere opportunity for your lower nature. You should be free to serve each other in love' (Galatians 5:13 PHILLIPS, italics mine).

As Christ comes into our lives at conversion the Holy Spirit is then free to take up the work of re-directing our whole being towards our rightful destiny, which is 'to be conformed to the image of his Son' (Romans 8:29). The image of God in man, damaged by Adam and Eve's violation in the Garden of Eden, now has to be rebuilt in the image of Christ. At conversion Christ is resident in our lives, but in order to enjoy spiritual freedom we must make sure that he is not only resident, but president. To the extent that we allow him to preside over our lives—to that extent can we be free.

We saw that at conversion Christ came in to take up his position as Lord in the centre of our existence, but in order to enjoy the full effect of his power and presence we must allow him to penetrate the whole of our being—our thoughts, our emotions and our will. William Law, the deep thinker of the eighteenth century said, '*A Christ not in us is a Christ not ours.*' In order to effect conformity to his character Christ offers us the gift of himself living at the centre of our being; thinking, feeling and willing within our hearts. Henry Scougal explained it like this: 'He diffuseth Himself through all their faculties and animates them with His life and Spirit that they may have no will or affections of their own, no desires or inclinations different from His, but that every pulse may answer to the motions of His heart and all their powers be actuated and enlivened by His Spirit—in a word, that it be no more they but Christ that liveth in them.'

The death and resurrection of Jesus Christ did not automatically deliver us from the bondage of the lower nature. He made his freedom available through divine conditions. As we allowed Christ to come in at conversion, so we must allow him to penetrate every area of our lives and free us from the bondage that carnality brings.

## It's impossible

In Romans 7, Paul came to the conclusion that he could not live the Christian life in the energy of his own natural enthusiasm, and it was only when he looked at Christ and saw the secret in him that he turned from despondency to delight.

A modern-day Christian explained it like this: 'At first,' he said, 'I thought the Christian life was *easy.* A little later on I came to see that it was *difficult.* Finally I became so frustrated that I discovered it was *impossible.* Then in my despair I turned from my self-effort to Christ and found that the Christian life was not my responsibility, but rather my response to his ability.' Just as Paul (and countless others) came to the conclusion that the Christian life is letting Christ relive his life within ours, so you too must face this fact if you are to function as God designed.

It might help us to grasp this thought more clearly if we ask ourselves, 'What was the secret of Christ's relationship with his Father when he was here upon this earth?' It can be summed up in one phrase—*complete submission.* The success of Christ's life was his utter dependence upon his Father who worked in and through him by the power of the Holy Spirit. In every situation he related it to his Father's ability and responded to God's will with enthusiasm and joy. 'The Son can do nothing of himself, but what he seeth the Father do,' he told the people who accused him of healing on the sabbath (John 5:19).

The apostle John went further to explain that as Christ walked through this world with his focus of attention on his Father, so are we to walk with our focus on Christ who will work through us to the glory of his name. 'He that saith he abideth in him ought himself also so to walk, even as he walked' (1 John 2:6). As God lived through Christ so he longs to live in us. He wants to think through our thoughts as he did through Jesus. He wants to speak through our lips as he did through Jesus. He wants to love through our hearts, as he did through Jesus.

## Christ in me

This then is the beating heart of it all. Christ in us, living at the centre of our being, manifesting his power throughout every area of our lives. There are many ways to say it: F. B. Meyer called it, 'The exchanged life'; A. B. Simpson termed it 'the larger life'; Watchman Nee titled it 'the normal Christian life' while Ruth Paxson called it 'life on the highest plane'. By far the best expression comes from the pen of the apostle Paul, 'I am crucified with Christ: nevertheless I live; yet not I, but Christ liveth in me: and the life which I now live in the flesh I live by the faith of the Son of God, who loved me, and gave himself for me' (Galatians 2:20).

Doesn't that take a great load off our personalities? No frantic effort or grinding struggle—simply letting Christ live his life within our beings. It is not so much imitation of Christ but participation in Christ.

What happens to a person who allows Christ to have absolute control? He enjoys (among other things) a spiritual freedom which enables him to move through life with poise, with dignity and with power. Christ's personality so penetrates his own that he needs less and less to pull his will into harmony with Christ's. The two wills mingle and move as one, and whenever the two wills threaten to pull apart then Christ's will prevails. If others want to boast with Henley that they are master of their fate then the surrendered Christian recognizes he is not of that number. He is content for Christ to be both Master and Lord, and into his nail-pierced hands he delights to entrust his soul.

Then what of the carnal Christian? He, on the other hand, allowing self to be in control, experiences conflict, bondage and despair. He is a fragmented person trying to make the best of both worlds. Jack Taylor described him in this way: 'This is how the carnal man makes decisions. He calls all his fragmented selves to a committee meeting. He has a religious self, a social self, an economic self, a family self, and others. The main business comes up for consideration. He seeks to "chair the board" but no one seems to agree. Whatever is under consideration, his various "selves" pull in the direction of their own interests.

What seems to be best religiously is a poor move financially. A decision is reached but it is never unanimous. He has sought to have a *democracy* in his inner life. What he needs is a Christocracy (total Christ rule).'

When Christ has complete control of a person's thought, emotions and will this fact will be evidenced by the appearance of nine major qualities in his life. Paul lists them in his epistle to the Galatians, 'But when the Holy Spirit controls our lives he will produce this kind of fruit in us: love, joy, peace, patience, kindness, goodness, faithfulness, gentleness and self-control' (Galatians 5:22-23 TLB).

'Now I'm confused,' you might say, 'If the secret is Christ living in me, then how does the Holy Spirit come into the picture?'

## The Holy Spirit is at work

Let's see if we can bring a few facts into closer focus. The Holy Spirit takes up residence in our personalities the moment we receive Christ. In fact Romans 8:9 says that not to have the Holy Spirit means that you are not a Christian in the New Testament sense at all: 'Now if any man have not the spirit of Christ, he is none of his.' A comparison of 1 Peter 1:11 and 2 Peter 1:21 will show you that the 'Spirit of Christ' and the 'Holy Spirit' are synonymous terms.

The main purpose of the Holy Spirit's indwelling in us at conversion is (as we have seen) so that we become 'conformed to the image of his Son' (Romans 8:29), and this process begins from the moment we receive Christ. Just as the Holy Spirit worked in the life of Christ when he was here on earth, to produce the qualities we see in him in the gospels, so he desires to work with Christ in our lives to produce conformity to Christ's likeness and image. Quite simply the Holy Spirit indwells us from conversion to produce the purity of Christ which shows itself in our lives in the nine major ways we have described above.

What then is the 'baptism of the Spirit', and how does this fit into God's plans for our lives? As the Holy Spirit comes in to *indwell* us at conversion, so there is a further experience of the Spirit whereby he comes *upon* us to supply that supernatural empowerment which we need for service in the world and through Christ's church. The second phase will be the subject of another part of this book, but right now we are discussing that aspect of the Holy Spirit's ministry which is related to producing purity in our lives.

As Christ lives in us and is allowed to have full control of our whole being, he is then free with the assistance of the Holy Spirit to deepen our characters, overcome the inner conflicts and lift our lives to that stage of overcoming that we call 'the abundant life'. Paul makes reference to a phrase in Romans 8 that sums this up completely: 'For the law of the spirit of life in Christ Jesus hath made me free from the law of sin and death' (Romans 8:2). *The law of the spirit of life*—what does he mean?

Just as there is a law of sin and death that produces spiritual bondage, so there is a law of life which produces liberty and freedom, and this 'law of the spirit of life' is available to all those who are 'in Christ'. Plant a bulb upside down! What is the result? The law of life inside it will cause it to turn a somersault as it struggles upwards towards the light. Hold this book out at arm's length, let it go, and what will happen? The law of gravity will pull it down to the floor. You could if you wished prevent it from reaching the floor by interposing your other hand, thereby introducing a law of suspension that would stop it in its downward path and overcome the law of gravity.

What then is the secret of overcoming the downward

pull of the carnal nature? It is simply letting Christ live his life in me! I must stop fighting, stop struggling and refuse to go on in the energy of the flesh. As I 'let go and let God' he will take over, and through the 'law of the spirit of life' will sustain me every single moment of my day.

Once there lived another man within me,
  Child of earth and slave of Satan he;
But I nailed him to the cross of Jesus,
  And that man is nothing now to me.

Now another Man is living in me,
  And I count his blessed life as mine;
I have died to all my own life,
  I have risen to all his life divine.

# 5

# *Maintaining a Clear Conscience*

It had been an exceptionally busy day in my office on the fourth floor of a building in Oxford Street, London, and I was eagerly looking forward to a quiet evening at home. Just as I was about to step into the lift that would take me down to street level, I heard someone behind me panting breathlessly, and a voice said, 'Don't go please—I have to see you urgently.'

I turned to find a young couple somewhere in their late twenties, standing at the top of the stairs.

'My wife wouldn't go in the lift,' the man said, 'and we had to come up this way,' pointing to the long flight of steps. 'I'm glad we caught you,' he continued, 'As we have come thirty miles to get here. Tomorrow my wife has to go into a mental institution and I brought her along to ask you if you would pray for her, please.'

Unlocking the door of my office I mentally said goodbye to a quiet evening at home and settled down to listen to the background of the problem. As the husband, who identified himself as Arthur, began the story, I kept one eye on his wife who appeared to be taking no interest whatsoever in what he was saying. Jean, he told me, had been acting rather strange lately and appeared to be 'mentally sick'. At this point his wife Jean began wringing her hands in a washing motion, accompanied by low moans which I must say caused me some alarm.

'Don't worry,' said Arthur. 'This is how she has been acting over the past few weeks. She doesn't do anything violent, but I can't get through to her, and there is no way that I can communicate what is happening.'

Jean was obviously in the grip of a serious psychosis and I wondered just what I should do about the situation. I have always been very cautious about counselling anyone described as 'mentally sick' and as the psychosis was so serious that it cut off communication, I felt a little inadequate for the situation.

'I wonder, can I talk to her alone for a few minutes?' I said to Arthur. He immediately agreed and retired to another room to wait and pray.

The moment Arthur left the room Jean appeared to relax, and it was not long before I was able to engage her in some conversation. I asked her about her family, her home, the children and other small talk, until I felt I was able to lead in to the one question I was longing to ask. At the right moment I placed it before her—very nervously I must admit—but sincerely seeking to discover the root cause of her conflict.

'Is there anything you have done that is causing you concern?' I have put that simple question to many people over the years but I have never seen a reaction such as I saw with Jean that moment. She began to shake violently, and flew at me, her fingers reaching out to scratch at my face, but I warded off her action and forced her to sit back down in her chair. She began to sob uncontrollably for about fifteen minutes, after which she sat quite still and lifeless in the chair, with her head in her hands.

I said nothing more until she looked at me with a pained expression and said, 'Why did you ask me if I had done anything wrong?' I pointed out that those were not my exact words and put the question again, exactly as I had said it the first time: 'Is there anything that you have done that is causing you concern?'

After several minutes of silence the story came out. Jean had been carrying on a secret adulterous affair with a man in her neighbourhood, which led to the development of several serious conflicts in her life resulting in her deep psychotic condition. I advised her to clear up the matter immediately, and with her permission I called Arthur into the room to hear the whole sad story.

He was shattered of course, but after several hours of discussion and prayer the whole matter was cleared up, forgiveness sought and received, and Jean and Arthur left my office just as Big Ben in the distance started striking the midnight hour.

Jean presented herself to the medical authorities the following day and was given a clean bill of health. Her psychosis disappeared and within days she had become a happy housewife and a devoted mother. I am not suggesting of course that the way to deal with 'mental sickness' is to ask the sufferer, 'Is there anything you have done which is causing you some concern?', but I have found in dealing with *some* cases that the basic problem is often a deep sense of guilt. Once this is removed the symptoms often disappear and the person concerned is able to take his place in society as a normal and responsible individual.

## The problem of guilt

Psychiatrists and therapists of all schools recognize that feelings of guilt can lead to serious types of neuroses and psychoses. Some seek to neutralize those feelings with expensive sessions of psychoanalysis, and it is understandable why many Christians have developed an aversion to the kind of therapy based on Freud's anti-scriptural presuppositions. Fortunately in more recent years a number of authorities have appeared who have parted company with conventional psychiatry, and who adopt approaches more in harmony with Christian principles.

One of the foremost of these is Dr William Glasser, who has presented his views in a powerful book entitled *Reality Therapy.* Glasser maintains that most emotional disturbances stem from a conscience that has been violated, and advocates therapy that attempts to deal with the guilt itself rather than pursuing the guilt feelings.

When God designed us in the beginning he equipped us for success and made no provision for us to live comfortably under the emotional strain of guilt. Guilt is therefore an imposition on our personalities which God never intended us to have. Someone has defined it in this way: 'Guilt is God's way of saying, "you have broken one of my principles."'

No Christian can enjoy complete freedom of mind until he has experienced a complete release from the burden of guilt. At conversion the burden of guilt is removed and, provided the repentance is complete, there follows a feeling something like the effect of a tranquillizer, only with this difference—the relief is immediate, more dramatic, permanent and free from hangovers.

'God,' says a well known Christian doctor, S. I. McMillen, 'is only obligated to give love, joy, and peace to those who yield themselves in total surrender to his will.'

## What is conscience?

Before we understand how to maintain our Christian lives in a position of permanent spiritual freedom we have to look in detail at a part of our personality which the Bible calls a 'conscience'. It is basically a compound word consisting of *con* meaning 'in conjunction with' and *science* meaning 'knowledge'. It is therefore knowledge held in conjuction with another—the other being God. Conscience plays such an important part in our lives as Christians that it has been described as the key to moral and spiritual freedom. There can be no doubt that spiritual achievement is measured by the transparency we have in our spirits towards God, ourselves and others.

How then do we go about gaining a transparent conscience?

First let's look at how it functions in our lives. At creation God built into us a special alarm system which was intended to ring whenever we crossed the limits God had set for us. The first man, Adam, violated God's instructions and doubtless when he did this, the warning bell rang inside him, but ignoring it he pressed on to take of the forbidden fruit. Immediately he sinned, his violated conscience protested against his action and produced an awareness of personal responsibility before God. It was because of this that Adam and Eve hid from God in the garden and attempted to cover their nakedness with leaves.

As the human system was not made to carry guilt some effort had to be made to deal with the emotional strain that occurred. Adam proceeded to rationalize his guilt by blaming the woman that God had given him, and by covering his nakedness with his own effort. As they reach the stage of an awareness of guilt, human beings respond either negatively or positively, according to their desires and values.

## A right response

The proper way to respond to the demands of an outraged conscience is by an act of complete repentance. Unless this happens the inner release which comes through pardon and forgiveness can never be experienced, and the person concerned is left with feelings of insecurity and despair. Some try to compensate for such a situation by attempting to deal with the pain of guilt in some other way. They become full of good works, generous in their giving to charitable causes, or make a religious profession without a true experience.

Responding correctly to the appeal of a sensitized conscience is a major way of progress in the Christian life. The power of a clear conscience is seen everywhere in the Bible. Here are just a few of the statements the Bible gives relating to this strategic matter:

'When a person is still living on milk it shows he isn't very far along in the Christian life, and doesn't know much about the difference between right and wrong' (Hebrews 5:13 TLB).

'Cling tightly to your faith in Christ and always keep your conscience clear, doing what you know is right' (1 Timothy 1:19 TLB).

'A man who refuses to admit his mistakes can never be successful. But if he confesses and forsakes them, he gets another chance' (Proverbs 28:13 TLB).

## Keeping conscience clear

Maintaining a clear conscience is one of the most important aspects of Christian experience. Day by day we should check on every possibility that we have hurt God or anyone else and as soon as any violation or infraction is apparent we should then, *without delay* put the matter right, whether it involves God, his church or others. As Satan knows the power that flows from a clear conscience, he will do all in his power to prevent you taking the necessary action to maintain its transparency. It will require a great deal of self-determination to check on violations, so here is a list which might help you walk with God with no unconfessed sin in your life and a clear conscience towards God, yourself and others.

You must ask yourself:

*Have I lied to anyone and never taken steps to correct it?* A lie pressing upon your conscience can damage your potential for Jesus Christ and enables Satan to have an unfair advantage over you. He will use the uncorrected violation time and time again to remind you of your below-standard Christian experience, and this in turn will hinder your effectiveness and curb your zeal in the things of God.

*Have I stolen anything from anyone and never remedied the matter?* Your honest answer to this question may lead you to attempt the restitution of hundreds (perhaps thousands) of pounds or just a few pence. Knowing the longing of a truly penitent heart to make amends (though this of course cannot wash away our sin) God will guide and work amazing miracles for those who are willing to follow him in this way. Don't be tempted to think only of the large things. What about the postage stamps you may have taken, or the telephone calls you have made on someone else's phone which still need to be paid.

*Have I lost my temper with anyone and not yet apologized?* It is interesting to go through the excuses the ill-tempered give to themselves and (occasionally) to others. Some put it down to temperament, indigestion, tiredness: while others blame it on their parents. 'My mother had a temper,' they say, and for reasons such as these Christians hide from the truth concerning themselves. There is no excuse for bad temper. Every alibi breaks down at the cross. Remember, when you apologize, don't say, 'I was wrong, but so were you too.' Bear your part of the blame without reference to the other person's responsibility.

*Have I damaged the reputation of anyone and failed to take the proper steps to correct it?* Jealousy and envy are the common causes for a situation like this. It is one of the saddest problems in Christian experience and fruitful of enormous harm. Pride will come to your aid and attempt to prevent you from taking the steps to correct the damage, but press through, for although pride will excuse your failure, God will work with you to overcome it.

*Have I grieved God (and others) by my ingratitude?* How often we receive favours of others without so much as a thank-you. Your minister preaches a sermon that meets deep into your need and you pass him by without a word of sincere and heartfelt appreciation. Your wife (or mother) cooks a meal that is a pleasure to eat but you leave the table with no word of praise. A young man I know won his mother and father to Christ by going to them after a soul-searching session in one of our seminars and saying, 'Mum, Dad, I have never ever said thank you for the way that you have brought me up. I want to do that now. Thank you for making me the man I am through your careful and loving upbringing.' Thank God regularly for all the blessings of life and be ready always to express gratitude to others around you who help you on life's way.

*Have I held bitterness and resentment against anyone and refused to forgive?* Bitterness and resentment are the major causes of unhappiness in our Christian lives. It breeds depression and disease, causes nervous breakdowns and mental unbalance, and freezes the river of joy in a Christian's soul. As long as we harbour an unforgiving spirit we cannot expect to be fully forgiven ourselves. This is a principle which Christ made clear in the prayer he framed for his disciples on the Mount of Olives. 'Your heavenly Father will forgive you if you forgive those who sin against you; but if *you* refuse to forgive them, *he* will not forgive *you*' (Matthew 6:14-15 TLB).

*Have I rebelled against the authority of someone over me (at work, school, church or home)?* God has shown us in his word that submission to authority over us is a mark of spiritual maturity. A failure to respect authority will lead to a violated conscience, and this in turn affects and damages the potential of our Christian witness. It might mean that you will have to go to an employer, a parent, a schoolteacher, and say, 'I am sorry for the way that I have not respected your authority. I see now I was wrong. Will you forgive me?'

*Have I committed fornication, adultery, or any other sexual sin and not yet sought forgiveness?* Sexual or sensual sins can, if not confessed, lead to a desensitized conscience. Avoidance of responsibility in this area can eventually, if persisted in, lead to conscience being seared, so that it will cease to work properly and thus become an ineffective part of our personality. Any act of sin should be cleared up *immediately*. Spiritual freedom stems only from a *clear* conscience.

*Have I violated God's laws by dabbling in fortune-telling, spiritism, playing with the ouija board or other devices?* The word *occult* means 'hidden' and, if at any time you have penetrated beyond that veil which God has marked 'keep out', you have violated his word and will need to confess your sin, repent of it, and ask for God's forgiveness. Over and over again in counselling sessions I have been forced to deal firmly with Christians who regard occult involvement as something that simply happened in the past, and have never taken the steps to close the door to Satan and demonic forces by a definite act of renunciation. It is not enough to obtain God's forgiveness. Shut the door firmly in Satan's face by saying, 'I renounce you and all your works and want nothing to do with you ever again. I bind your power in the name of Jesus Christ, and command you to obey the authority of the Son of God who overcame you on the cross of Calvary.'

Becoming a mature Christian depends on the skill and speed by which we handle our problems as they arise within our lives. The simple secret of a life free from bondage and despair is to act *instantly* we recognize that one of God's principles has been violated. Guilt, when repressed and allowed to remain in the mind, will only store up trouble for later on.

*A clear conscience should be the constant aim of every Christian.* Without it we are like ships with a faulty compass trying desperately to chart a course through troubled seas.

Let the apostle Paul have the last word on this vital issue: he says you are sent into battle 'for the right armed only with your faith and a *clear conscience.* Some, alas, have laid these simple weapons contemptuously aside and, as far as their faith is concerned, have run their ships on the rocks' (1 Timothy 1:18-19 PHILLIPS).

# 6

# *Feeling Guilty about Feeling Guilty*

Diana, a thirty-year-old minister's wife, rose to her feet as I entered the counselling room, and before I had time to greet her with the customary handshake, she blurted out, 'Oh please help me; I'm ruining my husband's ministry and if something doesn't change soon he is going to have to give up the church. Do you think you can help me? I hope so, because if you can't I don't know what I'm going to do. Is there any hope for someone like me?'

'Diana,' I said, 'I'm sure God has a solution to your problem, but before we try to find it let's sit down and have a word of prayer together. It's important, if we are to receive God's answer to the problem, that we be in the right frame of mind. I think a word of prayer will help us achieve that—do you agree?' Diana nodded her head furiously, and so I prayed a simple prayer that went something like this: 'Lord, we are so thankful that for every problem and difficult situation we face in life, you have a clear answer to it. Help us, as we talk together and listen to each other, to listen for your voice too. Be with us now in a very special way as Diana shares her problem. In Jesus' Name. Amen.' After this brief prayer Diana seemed a little more composed, and so I said, 'Now, how can I help you?'

'Well, things came to a head last Saturday,' she began.

'It was such a beautiful day that my husband decided to leave the children with friends and take me for a drive into the country. Everything was fine until we stopped for lunch at a small roadside restaurant: then, right in the middle of the meal, I began to feel depressed, so much so that I started to cry. It was all so embarrassing because my husband had to take me back to the car, apologize to the people who ran the restaurant, and then drive me home.'

'What do you think caused the depression, Diana?' I asked. 'Oh, I know what caused it all right,' she said. 'I felt guilty that I had dragged my husband away from his work and his duties, to take me out into the country. There were ever so many things he needed to do to prepare for the weekend, and I let him take me for a ride when he could have been better occupied.'

'I might have misunderstood you, Diana,' I said, 'but I got the impression from what you said that it was your husband who volunteered to take you for a ride, and not because of a suggestion from you.' 'Yes, that's true,' she responded, 'and that's my problem. I feel guilty about almost everything I do, and then when I feel guilty, *I feel guilty about feeling guilty.'*

'Tell me a little more about the problem and how it affects you,' I said. 'What are some of the situations that cause these guilty feelings to emerge?'

'Well,' she responded, beginning to twist her handkerchief nervously. 'Take this situation, for example. If I oversleep and I can't have my usual thirty-minute "quiet time", I feel so dreadfully guilty about it that I can hardly cope. It's not so much because I have missed a quiet time—I know in my head God understands that—but I feel such a failure in my heart. On such occasions I am impossible to live with. Then there are those occasions when my husband preaches a challenging message in church. Every time he does that I feel as if I'm not doing enough for the Lord. It actually seems as if inside me there is a slave driver with a whip, urging me forward, and saying, "You *ought* to do better. You *ought* to do better." Every week I am trying to do more for the Lord, more for the church and more for my family, and all I seem to be succeeding in doing is knocking myself out. I just can't go on like this any longer. I seem to be trapped.'

I explained to Diana that her problem was not an unusual one and that in the Christian church there were thousands more like her who carried inside them what is sometimes described as 'feelings of pseudo-guilt'. They feel guilty about things which they shouldn't feel guilty about, and go through life punishing themselves for things which God regards as unimportant. In the previous chapter we dealt with the need to develop a conscience that is sensitive to the Holy Spirit, so that whenever a scriptural principle is violated we can immediately recognize it and put it right. Diana's problem, one that in my experience affects a multitude of Christians, was not that her conscience was *under*-sensitive, but that it was *over*-sensitive. Her conscience condemned her over matters which God undoubtedly regarded as trivial. The insights and suggestions I shared with Diana that day (and also in further counselling sessions that were spread over several weeks) seemed to help her greatly and, although it took three to four months before, with God's help, she was able to shake herself free of her pseudo-guilt feelings, she became a different person from the one who faced me in the initial counselling session.

Once we grasp and comprehend the way to handle feelings of pseudo-guilt, we are on the way to real living. Some of the insights I shared with Diana that day regarding her problem I propose to share with you now.

## Three kinds of guilt

In order to understand the whole subject of guilt we must recognize that in human life and existence it takes three forms—civil guilt, theological guilt and psychological guilt. Let's examine each of them in turn.

*Civil guilt* is the violation of human law. When we exceed the speed limit, for example, or park our car in a clearly forbidden zone, we are guilty of breaking the law. At such times we may not *feel* we are breaking the law, or experience any sense of guilt, but the lack of feeling makes no difference to the issue. We may not feel guilty when roaring up the motorway at ninety miles an hour, but we are guilty nevertheless. Some, of course, will have a sense of uneasiness when violating the law, but feelings have little to do with this issue. Civil guilt is an objective fact.

*Theological guilt* is the violation of divine law. Again this is largely an objective fact. Some people might feel guilty about breaking God's laws, while others might not. But regardless of how we feel, or how we don't feel, the Bible teaches that we are all guilty before God. The apostle Paul, in his epistle to the Romans, says, 'All have sinned, and come short of the glory of God' (Romans 3:23). Every man and woman born into this world from Adam's day to this—with the single exception of our Lord Jesus Christ—is a sinner. You are a sinner: I am a sinner. We are all sinners in God's sight, having violated his commandments, sought to manage our own affairs, and rejected God's offer of salvation.

*Psychological guilt* or pscudo-guilt as it is somctimes called, is the violation of self-established law in our conscience. It is not objective but subjective and *always* causes painful feelings. It is the awful realization: 'I have failed; I ought to have done better; I am guilty.' These feelings that plague people are not of a spiritual nature but instead result from emotional and environmental causes. A person like Diana can know the experience of conversion through which all past sin is forgiven, and yet be unable to remove the feelings of guilt and dread which linger in the personality. This prompts us to ask the question: 'How does pseudo-guilt arise, and what causes it to pervade so many personalities?'

## The birth and development of pseudo-guilt

In a counselling seminar a leader invited the group to answer the pointed question: what do you experience when you feel guilty? Their answers were very revealing and reflected a wide range of inner emotions. Here are some of the responses.

> 'I'm scared of what lies ahead.'
> 'My mind has a tendency to kick itself.'
> 'I have a feeling of impending punishment.'
> 'I feel a complete failure.'
> 'I feel unworthy and inferior.'
> 'I feel dirty or stained.'
> 'I feel terrible—like nobody loves me—especially God.'
> 'I feel dislike for myself—not accepted.'
> 'I don't want to show my face to people.'

These statements reflect three powerful feelings: (1) a fear of punishment; (2) a sense of worthlessness; and (3) a feeling of rejection and isolation. These three emotions, in fact, form the core of pseudo-guilt feelings. Whenever we feel guilty in the psychological sense we are actually experiencing an internal fear of punishment, a sense of unworthiness, or a fear of alienation and rejection. But how do such feelings develop, and how do they get such a grip upon the personality? And why do some adults experience such guilt so much more strongly than their neighbours? To answer these questions we have to look a little more closely at the influences which shape our emotional lives: it is only then that we can begin to unravel the cords of binding guilt.

## The ideal self

A psychologist by the name of Bruce Narramore has put forward the idea that psychological guilt develops because of a wrong relationship between what he calls our ideal self, our punitive self and our loving corrective self. Let me try to pull the whole concept into focus for you.

The *ideal self* is that part of our personality which develops soon after birth—the part which contains our ideals, our goals and our aspirations. Our parents, for example, establish expectations. They expect us to be smart, pretty, well mannered, polite, athletic, talented and obedient. We are taught to say 'please', to stop fighting with our brothers and sisters, to keep our room tidy, and a hundred other things. Each family has its own set of aspirations and expectations. Some families place a high value on athletic ability. Others pride themselves on social skills, academic attainment or financial prosperity. In addition to parental influences we learn other values from our environment. Television and the media project a variety of distorted images to a growing child. The 'successful' person on television is pretty or handsome, intelligent, athletic, personable and suave. Consciously or unconsciously the media presentations and other influences, such as peer pressures and ideas, merge with the ideals of our parents and teachers and are absorbed into our personality. They come together to form a picture, a mental image, of what we think we want, or ought to be, and once these thoughts crystallize this set of expectations and aspirations becomes our ideal self. It is the self we believe will make us happy and contented if we can only reach it. It becomes the standard by which we judge ourselves and our performance. If we meet our ideal standards we tend to like ourselves, and we experience what psychologists call self-esteem. But when, for some reason, we fall short of our ideals, we are left with feelings of discouragement or dissatisfaction. This ideal self, which is formed in early childhood, becomes a solid fixture in our personalities, and when we become adults we tend to continue to judge ourselves by the standards we absorbed as children and young adults.

## The punitive self

In addition to the ideal self another self is forming in the personality—the punitive self. Just as we take in the ideals, goals and expectations of our parents, so we absorb their methods of discipline. If our parents repeatedly said 'Shame on you', 'You're a bad boy (or girl)', 'You idiot!', 'You stupid child', we soon learn to repeat these statements to ourselves whenever we fall short of our expectations. Diana told me during the time we spent together in counselling that she often caught herself talking to herself in the same phrases that her mother used when correcting or reprimanding her. One of them was 'You foolish girl'. Isn't it a fact that we sometimes scold ourselves as adults with the exact words and tone of voice our parents used?

In most households whenever a child falls short of the standards set, or does something which deserves discipline, he is told, 'Because you did that, you must be punished.' The child gradually comes to learn that when he falls short of parental standards he can expect punishment. Soon there is established in his thought patterns the expectation: 'When I do wrong in my parents' eyes *I deserve to be punished.'* While this thought is to be expected and is quite natural, it is also the root cause of neurotic guilt feelings. Just as parents attack a child's self-esteem when he fails to live up to their standards, so the child, when he becomes an adult, applies the same discipline to himself and berates himself for falling short. If his parents used harsh, reprimanding and strongly punitive words and phrases when disciplining him, then he will tend to discipline himself in this same way.

A woman once told me that whenever she was disappointed with herself over some issue, she had to resist the temptation to cut herself with a sharp knife or razor blade. As we talked, it became apparent that ringing in her personality was the punitive tones of harsh and unloving parents which she was applying to herself in an abnormal way. The insight she gained when this was discussed was strong enough to enable her to handle any further problems that came her way. To the degree that our parents used harsh, demanding, unloving, judgemental and punitive attitudes and tones, to that degree we tend to exercise our punitive self whenever we fall short of our internalized standards and ideals.

## The loving-corrective self

We ought to be thankful that the negative and punitive messages we receive from our parents are only one side of the coin. Most parents know how to give positive, as well as negative input into the lives of their children, and in contrast to the harsh, judgemental attitudes of the punitive self they dispense encouragement, love, acceptance and support. If parents lean more towards harshness and criticism when disciplining their children than they do towards acceptance and encouragement, then the child tends in later life to follow that method in relation to his own mistakes and failures. Picture a home where both parents know how to give correction and discipline in a kind and loving manner. When the child fails and comes short of their expectations he is corrected, but in such a way that he still feels loved, accepted and valued for what he is. He knows that his parents understand his anxieties, his frustrations and his fears, and that they are correcting him in a way that will enable him to cope with his failures and his mistakes in the future. What happens in the personality of a child who develops under the training and guidance of such loving and accepting parents? When he becomes an adult he finds that he has internalized the same set of loving, corrective attitudes which his parents displayed towards him, so that when, as an adult, he fails or makes a mistake, he says to himself, 'This mistake (or failure) is something I regret, but it is not devastating. God loves me despite my failures, and has a wonderful plan for my life. He will give me the inner strength and resources to cope with my failure and to turn it to good. I know I cannot be a fully developed Christian overnight and that there will be times when I will fail, but because God loves me and is sovereign he will enable me to take my failures and turn them into stepping stones. Because of this I will press on and look to him to give me the strength and wisdom to turn this stumbling block into a springboard.'

## The conscience

Another important factor we have to consider in the birth and development of guilt is that of conscience. We have already looked at the subject of conscience in the previous chapter, but now we must view it from a slightly different angle. Conscience is not, by itself, a complete moral system. The word, as we saw, means co-knowledge; knowledge held in conjunction with another. When the conscience functions in relation to God then it functions as it was designed. The problem is, however, that our parents have access to our conscience before God does (in the sense of training it) and the way they deal with our conscience is crucial to our psychological growth and identity. This is why a child brought up with parents who build into its conscience unrealistic expectations and ideals sometimes finds, even after conversion, that parental influence continues to exert itself. And that influence, unless he has the insight to break away from it and knows how to handle it, can damage his spiritual potential.

Now, let's bring all this together into a concise and summarized statement. We all enter adult life with a set of goals and expectations which we call our ideal self. When we fall short of our ideals our conscience triggers an awareness of our failure and releases in our personality whatever corrective attitudes exist there. If the preponderance of our parents' corrective attitudes were harsh and judgemental, then our punitive self responds to our adult failures with a similar attitude of rejection—self-rejection. If, on the other hand, our parents accepted us, loved us, understood us, and when disciplining us made us feel valued for what we were as persons, and refrained from shaming or humiliating us, then we will respond to the falling short of our ideals in a positive and healthy way. We will be able to admit our failures without allowing ourselves to come under a great deal of self-condemnation and guilt. We will be ready to acknowledge our weaknesses and limitations, while maintaining our self-esteem and self-acceptance.

## Guilt must be punished

The whole problem of guilt deepens, of course, when we consider that God has designed the universe in such a way that guilt cannot go unpunished. 'There is within us,' says Dr Cecil Osborne, a Christian minister and psychologist, 'an inner mechanism which tends to enforce its own edict "confess or be punished".' Either we secure a sense of forgiveness in relation to guilt or else we will do two things with it—project it on to someone else and blame them (as did Adam in the garden of Eden) or punish ourselves. In Diana's case the depression she felt at the lunch table was in reality an attempt to punish herself for the guilt she felt for letting her husband take her on a day's outing. The depression was an attempt at self-punishment and served as a temporary release from guilt.

As God has constituted his universe and designed each human being with the intuitive knowledge that guilt must be punished, it is easy to see that when a person feels guilt, even pseudo-guilt, there are mechanisms that go to work in the personality to bring about a resolution of the issue. I am, at this moment, not so much concerned with an overt guilty act, but with all that registers on the inner self as guilt: shame, inferiority, feelings of rejection, self-despisings and worthlessness. We can punish ourselves quite as inexorably for false guilt as for real guilt.

A woman who had suffered with asthma most of her life told me, in answer to a question I put to her, that she was not aware of any unresolved guilt in her life, but as we talked, she shared with me a buried memory of being sexually assaulted as a small child. Unable to face the issue in her conscious mind she had repressed the event, not allowing it to come to the surface to be dealt with, until I gently faced her with the need to accept it, forgive the man who had assaulted her, and surrender the whole thing into God's hands. When she did this her asthma disappeared and, as far as I know, has never returned. A sense of shame over her childhood experience had settled upon her soul as guilt, but since she had not considered herself guilty of anything, it never occurred to her to deal with that particular experience. It was not God who condemned her, but some inner portion of herself; her own judicial system which was still pronouncing her 'guilty'. Unable to come to terms with the issue she subconsciously paid self-atonement by developing the psychosomatic problem of asthma, (of course, not all asthma is psychosomatic). When the matter was faced and dealt with, and her personality saw there was no further need for self-atonement as the guilt had gone, the asthma disappeared of its own accord.

## Pseudo-guilt is self-centred

Another important thing to observe in relation to psychological guilt (pseudo-guilt) is the fact that it is largely selfish and self-centred. Its real concern is not so much 'What have I done to others and how can I correct the harm I have done them?' but 'What a failure I am; what will everyone think of me?' Pseudo-guilt focuses largely on past failures, a sense of wrongdoing and a feeling of deserving punishment. Sometimes it masquerades as a concern for others but, when properly scrutinized, it is shown up for what it really is—self-centredness and egocentricity.

Picture two Christian women sitting together in a kitchen, chatting over a morning cup of coffee. Imagine one of them with an over-sensitive conscience who, when reaching for the sugar, accidentally knocks the other person's coffee into her lap. A typical reaction to this would be: 'How stupid of me. I should have known better. Look at the mess I've made. I'm so sorry. How will you ever forgive me?' Hours later she will still be feeling guilty and continue to berate herself. The focus here is very much on self and on past failure. A person with a properly balanced conscience, and good emotional adjustment, would react differently under the circumstances I have just described. She might say something like this: 'Oh, I'm so sorry. Please forgive me. Let me clean this table up. You will obviously have to get your skirt cleaned. I insist on paying the bill.' In a little while the matter would be forgotten because the focus being more on the other person than on oneself would be more healthy and realistic.

## Getting rid of guilt

How do we begin to differentiate between real guilt and pseudo-guilt? What steps do we need to take to ensure that we are not feeling guilty over things that God does not regard as sin? The first question we should ask ourselves whenever we feel a twinge of guilt is this: 'Am I feeling guilty because I have violated the standards of God's word, or because I have transgressed the childish standards of my ideal self?' If it is apparent that there has been a violation of a scriptural principle, then an effort should be made immediately to put things right. The principles of procedure in relation to the removal of theological guilt are clearly outlined in the previous chapter. What do we do, however, when we discover that the guilt we feel is pseudo-guilt and arises from a violation of our own internalized standards? Here is a digest of rules to follow when confronted by this problem:

*1. Face the fact that your inner personality mechanism needs to be realigned.* The long course of childhood training leaves deep imprints upon our personalities. Our ideal self, our punitive self, and our loving-corrective self, if not functioning correctly, will need to be brought into line with the Bible. We must learn to focus on God's expectations for our lives and to keep before us constantly and continuously the vision of God's pattern of parenthood. In the same way our punitive and loving-corrective self must change. We must learn that whenever God disciplines us it is because he loves us and that his corrections are never retributive, but remedial. People who are afflicted with the problem of false guilt invariably have a wrong concept of God. They see God as punitive, harsh, judgemental and demanding—a hangover from their past. Take the Scripture passages that show what God is really like, meditate upon them until they begin to bring about a realignment of your personality and refocus your vision on a true understanding of your loving heavenly Father.

2. *Throw a spotlight on your feelings as they arise and gain experience in classifying thoughts and feelings which come from past relationships.* One lady I spoke to some time ago told me that unless she always washed up immediately after a meal she would be plagued with feelings of guilt. As we talked, it became apparent that this arose from her relationship with her mother who insisted that once a meal was over the dishes should never be allowed to remain on the table for more than a few minutes, but should be taken to the sink and immediately washed. This repeated day-by-day procedure had formed part of her ideal self and when, for some reason such as tiredness or disinclination, she did not wash them right away, her conscience triggered off an alarm system in her personality and guilt descended upon her mind. When she saw what was happening, and recognized the root of her problem, she began to put into operation the principle I am now suggesting. She threw a spotlight on her feelings, challenged them, identified them, and recognized them for

what they were. She would put the dishes into the sink and say, 'There now, you will get washed when I am ready, and not before. I am not a slave. I am a free person and I refuse to be threatened or intimidated by you, or by anything out of my past.' After a few weeks of this she found that the sense of guilt gradually began to diminish and after a period of three months the issue did not trouble her any more. She was able to wash the dishes, or not wash the dishes, *as she chose*—no longer driven by an unhealthy emotional push from the past.

*3. Meditate on the Scriptures until the Bible's ideals become your ideals.* The psalmist said, 'Thy word have I hid in mine heart, that I might not sin against thee .... I will meditate in thy precepts, and have respect unto thy ways. I will delight myself in thy statutes: I will not forget thy word' (Psalm 119:11, 15-16). David said that he repeatedly meditated on God's instructions until they became an integral part of his personality. To put this into the phraseology we have been using in this chapter, David studied the Old Testament Scriptures (or the part available to him at that time) and gradually it became a part of his ideal self. The Bible corrected David's wrong concepts of what was good for him, and replaced them with the truth of God. We all, to some extent, need the correction of the Scriptures, for although God uses parents, and others, to instruct us, the only completely reliable source for our ideals is the Bible.

In the Bible we have some clear teaching on how to resolve the guilt feelings which come from our punitive-corrective self. Writing to the Christians in Rome, Paul says, 'I beseech you therefore, brethren, by the mercies of God, that ye present your bodies a living sacrifice, holy, acceptable unto God, which is your reasonable service' (Romans 12:1). Again, when writing to the Christians in Ephesus he stated, 'And you hath he quickened, who were dead in trespasses and sins. I therefore, the prisoner of the Lord, beseech you that ye walk worthy of the vocation wherewith ye are called. With all lowliness and meekness, with longsuffering, forbearing one another in love; endeavouring to keep the unity of the Spirit in the bond of peace' (Ephesians 2:1, 4:1-3).

Here Paul shows that the true motive for self-correction should flow out of the fact that God loves us. The great God of the universe, he says, has shown us such abundant mercy that in response to this love we ought to be willing to put off our former rebellious ways of life and humbly develop new patterns of thought and action. There is no suggestion in the New Testament of a harsh, punitive type of guilt-motivation on the part of the Almighty. The Scripture gives us clear instructions for self-correction, but it always sets the pattern in the context of God's love. This is why, when people say to me, 'My problem is that I don't love the Lord enough,' I always respond, 'No, that's not your problem: your problem is that you don't know how much the Lord loves you.' When we see, really see, how much God loves us, then this is all the motivation we need to serve him, obey him and share his love with a sin-soiled world.

*4. Accept the gap between what you are and what you should be as part of your future growth.* Christians who suffer from pseudo-guilt feelings are notorious for wanting instant solutions to their problems. They say to themselves, 'If I can get hold of that cassette tape, hear that famous speaker, attend that conference or rally... I'm sure my problem will be solved.' If you find yourself thinking like that, then recognize right now that although there are crisis experiences when God comes in and does wonderful things for us in answer to prayer, *growth* in the Christian life is usually steady and progressive. Remember you are a Christian 'in the making'. No one becomes a fully fledged Christian in a day, in a week, or even in a year. We grow in relation to the way we apply biblical principles to our lives, slowly, methodically and progressively.

What did Jesus say about the 'lilies'? 'Consider the lilies of the field, how they *grow*: they toil not, neither do they spin' (Matthew 6:28 italics mine). Just how does a lily grow? By struggling, by striving or by frantic effort? No; it simply absorbs the provision of its environment—the wind, the rain and the sun—and it grows without any strain. So set your eye on the goal of all Christian growth—God's expectation for you, contained in Romans 8:29, 'For from the very beginning God decided that [we] should become like his Son'—and, in moving towards that goal, recognize that although at times you will feel a failure, God still loves you, cares for you, understands you, and constantly pursues his loving and eternal purpose in your life.

5. *Ponder on the fact that as a Christian you are acceptable to God as you are—and stop trying to 'earn' God's approval.* A good deal of tension begins to flow out of our personalities when we come to see that there is no way we can be acceptable to God through self-effort alone—we are acceptable to God because of what Christ has done for us and because of our position in him. Paul, when writing to the Colossians, puts it beautifully and succinctly when he says, 'Ye are complete in him' (Colossians 2:10). When we rest on the truth that Christ has made us totally acceptable to God, we stop being Christian 'workaholics'—people trying to work at gaining God's approval—and, in turn, become relaxed Christians working *because* we are saved, rather than working in order *to* be saved. The difference between these two things is crucial to our inner peace and happiness.

It is important to see that God accepts you as you are. If

there were no positive changes in your life over the next five years God would still accept you as you are. His acceptance of you is not conditioned by your actions, or even by your growth, but by his unconditional love. But, although God loves you as you are, he loves you too much to let you stay as you are, and constantly seeks to bring your life into a closer likeness and identification with his Son, the Lord Jesus Christ.

In a Counsellor Training Course I was conducting, a man said to me during one of the sessions, 'Isn't it dangerous to tell Christians that God accepts them as they are? What motivation will they have for self-improvement if they accept that as a fact?' This provoked a lively discussion in the group, the conclusion of which was this: 'If we see that God accepts us as we are, and does not make our growth and development a condition of his acceptance, this frees us to be the people he wants us to be—those who mature in a healthy way and at a pace that brings honour and glory to his name. If we believe that God only accepts us on the basis of our development, we will be motivated to over-extend ourselves and will strive to "earn" his approval. But once we know we are totally acceptable to God we can relax, stop striving and trying to merit either his approval or our own, and begin to *enjoy* our Christianity, rather than *endure* it.'

That conclusion I most heartily endorse. I hope it becomes yours too!

# 7

# *Getting the Best from the Bible*

'I promise that I will not keep you more than a few minutes, sir, but I would be most thankful if you can help me over this one thing.' The speaker was a tall Indian schoolteacher who stood framed in the doorway of my hotel room in the city of Madras, South India.

I was in the city at the invitation of a group of churches to conduct a minister's seminar and an evangelistic crusade. The committee responsible for my invitation had invited me to give the early morning Bible studies in a large hall near the centre of the city, at which several thousand people gathered to listen to the exposition of the word of God before commencement of the day's work.

I had just returned to my hotel room from one of these sessions and was about to sit down to breakfast when my uninvited guest appeared in the doorway.

'I followed you back here, sir,' he went on, 'as I have been sitting in the Bible studies each morning and I wondered why it is that you find so much pleasure in the Bible when to me it is such a *dull* book.'

Inviting him into the room I offered him a seat, taking out of his hand the copy of the Bible he was holding.

'You obviously know something of the Bible,' I said, 'but let me ask you this—*do you know the Author?'*

Looking at me rather quizzically he said slowly, 'How

do you mean sir—know the Author!'

'The Bible,' I said, 'was not compiled by men, but by God. In order to understand it properly you have to know something about the Author, so may I ask you once again—do you know God in a personal way, or if you prefer, have you ever received Jesus Christ into your life as your Saviour and Lord?'

'I'm afraid I don't understand much about those things, sir,' was his reply. 'But I do try to live a good life, and I attend many religious meetings.'

Sensing his deep longing for reality I asked him quite simply, 'Would you now at this moment like to receive Jesus Christ into your life and become a *real* Christian?'

'Yes, sir,' he said 'but how does it take place?'

After the reading of a few carefully chosen Scripture passages, and a short explanation of how to admit Christ into his heart as Lord, he bowed his head and quietly surrendered his life to Jesus Christ.

I saw him again in several of the meetings during my stay in the city, but for some reason I was never able to get close enough to engage him in conversation and discover how his new found Christian experience was progressing. On the last day of the crusade, however, the ministers arranged a special farewell meal for me, and following the close of the ceremony I found myself standing near my friend who, catching my eye, walked over to me and gripped me by the hand to say goodbye.

'How is your Bible reading working out now,' I asked, 'since you came to know the Author?'

His eyes lit up with excitement and with a broad smile he remarked, 'Since that morning in your hotel room I have not been reading the Bible—*it has been reading me.* There are so many things I have had to put right in my life. It's more wonderful than any book I have ever known, sir. Since I came to know the Author of course.'

## Why some find the Bible dull

Many people, like my friend in the east, find the Bible a dull book. They are amazed when they hear of others being fascinated by its pages, and consider it unbelievable that people can spend endless hours of delight and fascination poring over its precepts and delving into its truths. How is it, you ask, that a book so boring to one can be so exciting to another?

It depends mainly on the way one approaches the Bible. If a man believes that the Scriptures are simply a collection of documents put together by writers who had no divine inspiration, then the book becomes like any other and deserves no exceptional respect or any special place in his heart. If on the other hand a man believes that the Bible is the word of God he will approach it with a reverence and respect, gaining a spiritual enrichment that will reach deep into his soul.

Once my Indian friend had committed himself to Christ and approached the Bible with a new look then the word came alive within his life and he found its message to be a constant prod and challenge to his heart. The real purpose of the Bible can be seen more clearly from one of the most sublime statements ever made by the apostle Paul.

Writing to his son in the faith, Timothy, he said, 'All scripture is given by inspiration of God and is profitable for doctrine, for reproof, for correction, for instruction in righteousness: that the man of God may be perfect, throughly furnished unto all good works' (2 Timothy 3:16-17). Incidentally if you want a pleasant evening browsing in your Bible try looking at all the 3:16's in the New Testament. I promise you an interesting hour!

## No ordinary book

The Bible is no *ordinary* book. It was inspired by the Holy Spirit, and because the Spirit was its *inspirer* he also has to become its *interpreter.* This will explain why a person who has never received Christ (and in whom the Holy Spirit therefore does not dwell) will find the Bible to be dull, uninteresting and the most boring of all books, but once he submits to Christ and receives him as Lord then immediately all this is changed. His spirit becomes alive to God and the Holy Spirit indwelling the sacred word unites with his spirit, bringing understanding and meaning from even its deepest truths.

The Scripture explains it in this way. 'But the man who isn't a Christian can't understand and can't accept these thoughts from God which the Holy Spirit teaches us. They sound foolish to him because only those who have the Holy Spirit within them can understand what the Holy Spirit means. Others just can't take it in.' (1 Corinthians 2:14-15 TLB).

The Holy Spirit produced the Bible for a very special purpose, which can be seen in the four phrases described by Paul in 2 Timothy 3:16.

*Doctrine*—the principles on which God wants our lives to run.

*Reproof*—the way in which God uses the Bible to show us when we are going wrong.

*Correction*—the steps given by God in his word to help us correct our personal failures.

*Instruction*—the clear teaching contained in the Scriptures which if adhered to will help keep us on God's track through time and into eternity.

## An instruction manual

We must stop thinking therefore of the Bible as a *sacrosanct* book or a sacred volume that has no application to this world. It is a sacred of course and divinely inspired, but its main purpose is to provide Christians with an *instruction manual* for daily living by which they can find guidance, instruction, correction and the special insights needed to live for God in a sin-soiled world.

Not only did God design us in the beginning for success, but he has gone even further by supplying us with a special manual of instruction so that we are able to trace immediately any breakdown or malfunction that will hinder us from functioning as God designed.

The God who authored this book made mankind, and one is made for the other as a key is made for a lock. Both were brought into being by the breath of God (Genesis 2:7; 2 Timothy 3:16). We must treat the Bible therefore as a manual and put it to workmanlike use. We can thumb it, mark it, wear it out and then simply buy another. What we must not do is place it on a high shelf and treat it with a distant reverence that makes it ineffective.

As a manual it shows us how to keep in perfect working order the various parts of our being, how to make spiritual repairs and how to maintain our whole personality in proper functioning order. It shows how to avoid abuse and use the product God has given to the best possible advantage.

When things go wrong in our lives we are so prone to pass the problem over to our doctor or psychiatrist. We take tension pills or sedatives and hope that this will be a way out of our problem. God, our great designer, knows the personality he made better than anyone in the universe. Bent, squeaky or run down parts are no problem to him, and in his instruction manual he has given us clear indications as to what we should do when anything goes wrong.

The Bible not only bears the stamp of divine authority, but it has a special *unity* too. Written by forty different writers over a period of fifteen hundred years, it carries a harmony and a unity that could only be achieved by a divine Author. Think of how *accurate* it is also. Over three hundred prophecies in the Old Testament relating to the Person of Jesus of Nazareth were all accurately fulfilled within the thirty-three years in which he lived on this earth. Someone has computed that the chance of over three hundred prophecies being fulfilled in the life of one person within the short span of thirty-three years is one in *eighty-three billion.*

Its *survival* throughout time is yet another miracle. Nineteen centuries have tested it. No book has been attacked and ridiculed as this one, but it has survived the fiercest opposition. Voltaire, the infidel, predicted that one hundred years after his death the Scriptures would be replaced by his writings. Only twenty-five years after his death the house in which he had written most of his works was occupied by a Christian organization and became the publishing house for the Geneva Bible Publishing Company.

In reading the Bible it is important to remember that the key to the Scriptures is Jesus Christ. As 'all roads lead to London' so every road in the Bible leads to the Son of God. All the Old Testament truths converge upon him; all the New Testament truths emerge from him. He is the core of the gospel. He is the centre of gravity of the Scriptures. He is the heart of the evangel.

## Ways to study the Bible

There are seven accepted ways of studying the Bible.

*Topical method*—taking a topic like faith, the Holy Spirit, redemption, and going through the Bible to find out what each Scripture reference has to say about that subject.

*Explanatory method*—reading a portion of Scripture using a Bible commentary to help explain its meaning.

*Cyclopedic method*—studying Scripture with the aid of a Bible dictionary which opens up the meaning of Bible words and phrases.

*Typical method*—explaining the types which illustrate things that relate to Christ, his church or other spiritual truths. One of the most fascinating of all the Bible's types is of course the *Tabernacle in the Wilderness* which is replete with illustrations of Christ and his work.

*Microscopic method*—taking a Bible word like 'justification' or 'santification' and looking at its inner meaning until every shade of the original word and its contextual relationship is scrutinized and understood.

*Telescopic method*—studying a whole book (preferably in a single sitting) viewing the scope of its content, its purpose, and its aim in an overall picture. Sometimes called 'getting a bird's eye view of the Bible', it is in fact a rewarding method of Bible study.

*Parallel method*—as one text in the Bible throws light upon another, a study of parallel text helps to unfold its true meaning (example: comparing James 5:7 with Deuteronomy 11:14). Most Bibles contain margin references which help the reader to follow this method.

Although there are seven accepted ways of studying the Bible there is only *one* way of taking its truth and translating it into spiritual energy. That way is by *meditation.*

Literally millions (yes I mean *millions*) fail to get the best out of their Bibles because they fail to put into operation the simple principles of Bible meditation. The Bible fairly bulges with promises of what will happen to us when we meditate, but these promises, in the main, are overlooked by the large majority of believers. Research in the United States revealed that only one Christian in ten thousand knew how to meditate. What similar research in Great Britain would reveal I can only conjecture, but I would imagine the figures to be just as disturbing. And all this when God has promised that meditation is the most powerful way of getting the best out of the Bible.

## Success dependent on meditation

It has been pointed out that God has promised success to Christians in proportion to their meditation in his word, and there are many Scripture statements that show how God relates spiritual progress to the continuous inner activity of meditation.

Here are just a few; there are of course many others.

'Thou shalt meditate therein day and night . . . for then thou shalt make thy way prosperous, and then thou shalt have good success' (Joshua 1:8).

'Meditate upon these things; give thyself wholly to them; that thy profiting might appear to all' (1 Timothy 4:15).

'Thy word have I hid in mine heart, that I might not sin against thee' (Psalm 119:11).

'O how I love thy law! It is my meditation all the day.... I have more understanding than all my teachers' (Psalm 119:97,99).

## The vital question

At this stage you may ask what precisely is meditation?

How do I go about putting it into practice in my Christian life and experience?

Meditation is the process by which we take a thought, a verse, or a passage from God's word, allow it to linger in our minds until it turns into spiritual form and energy. Just as food when received into the digestive system eventually becomes muscle, bone, and blood, so through meditation the word of God is transformed from biblical principles into spiritual reality.

The concept behind the word 'meditation' is that of a cow chewing a cud. Just as that which a cow has eaten is brought up again and again, so the word of God when recalled in the mind through the continuous inner activity of meditation will flush out thoughts opposed to Scripture and help construct our lives around the principles of the word of God.

At conversion God enters our lives through the power of the Holy Spirit and establishes within our spirits a living relationship with himself. Once the spirit has been made alive it needs to be fed, and the nourishment for the spirit is the word of God (1 Peter 2:2; Matthew 4:4). As God's Spirit unites with our spirit conscience is strengthened, our understanding of God is clarified and the creative drives (all part of the spirit) are directed and channelled towards himself. However, the mind continues to manifest conflicting thoughts, desires and emotions, which in turn produce deep inner conflict. Allowing the word of God to penetrate and infiltrate the mind is essentially the purpose of meditation.

No man is changed until his mind is changed. Most of our living is done from within and, as our deeds express our thoughts, the word of God must penetrate this area if our lives are to be like Christ's. The Bible shows the mind to be a powerful part of our personality. '*As a man thinks,*' says the Scripture, '*so is he*' (see Proverbs 23:7). No wonder Paul insisted, 'Let this mind be in you, which was also in Christ Jesus' (Philippians 2:5). Meditation enables the mind of Christ to flow into our minds, and the more we meditate the more of Christ's mind will be seen in us.

## The mind of Christ

There are nine components to the mind of Christ which you can read about in the New Testament, listed for us by the apostle Paul in his letter to the Galatians: 'But when the Holy Spirit controls our lives he will produce this kind of fruit in us: love, joy, peace, patience, kindness, goodness, faithfulness, gentleness and self-control' (Galatians 5:22 -23 TLB).

Wouldn't you like to have a mind like that? A mind free from nervous disorders, able to overcome evil thoughts, and wide open to the stream of God's eternal love and peace? All the components of the mind of Christ are yours! God said so! You cannot manufacture them or make them. You simply *let* them dwell in you through the process of meditation.

Here's how to get started in meditation.

*First* see quite clearly those aspects of the mind of Christ you lack. Each heart will discover its own need as the gaze is turned upon him. One will be convicted of resentment; one of fear; another of bitterness and another of lust. Now see these needs set over against the perfect character of Jesus Christ and realize that for fear he gives peace; for irritability he gives patience; for self-pity, courage and joy; for lust, self-control. The answer to your need lies in receiving the mind of Christ, and in first seeing with clarity those aspects of his mind which you most lack.

*Next* begin to 'covet earnestly' those aspects you need, with fervency and desire. But how does one do this? Feelings are not the slave of the will. When thought sees clearly the end in sight, and the conscience adds its approving testimony, how does one generate the enthusiasm and the desire so necessary to the achievement?

Some years ago one of my sons wanted a bicycle. It started when he looked into a shop window and saw it there, all bright and shiny. Day and night he lived with the thought of possessing that machine. It was the theme of all his conversations. He dreamt of it, talked of it, and ached to own it. He explained to his mother and I how it would save him the fares to school, and how much more quickly he could get his homework done, because he would be able to get home that much earlier... on and on the arguments went, until at last he possessed his bicycle. Such ardent desire seems always to get what it wants!

There appear to be laws in the universe that work for those who have a clear picture of what they want, then attach to it a burning desire for possession. When the end desired is God's end also, then all the power of God moves in that direction to help achieve it. Useful and necessary as material things are, what are they beside the components of the mind of Christ? Let me ask you once again: what is it worth to you to have a mind free from worry, anxiety, lust, or the power of evil thoughts? The desire for freedom will in itself be the motivation you need, and provide you with the longing to reach out and receive.

As you picture yourself in possession of the aspects of Christ's mind which you need, then the longing will grow in you even more. God designed you in the beginning to love these things, and all the help of your great designer is there to assist you.

*Now* select suitable passages of Scripture on which your mind can fasten to practise the art of meditation. Assuming that after gazing at the mind of Christ you feel that genuine love is your greatest lack, and having followed the first two steps mentioned above, find a portion of Scripture that relates directly to this problem and begin the process of meditation right away. With the need for genuine love the appropriate passage of course would be 1 Corinthians 13, and meditation on this chapter will help produce those deep qualities of which Paul so glowingly speaks.

If peace is your particular need, or if you are troubled by wrong thoughts, then choose a passage that relates to your problem and meditate upon it until it changes from a principle to a reality in your life.

The secret of meditation is to allow an appropriate Scripture to *linger* in your mind. It is not simply memorizing the Bible, but letting it *lie* in your thoughts hour after hour, day after day (if necessary), until the quality you seek begins to make itself apparent in your life. Learn to let the text or thought taken from Scripture leave your mind, then bring it back again, repeating this process over and over and over. The power of meditation lies in the 'striking' action of the word of God hitting against your own thought process, just as in a washing machine an agitator beats against the clothes until it washes away the impurities.

Remember the illustration of the cow chewing the cud? That's how meditation works in your spiritual being. You let the word lie in your mind, allow it to be temporarily forgotten (as when you are about other tasks), then bring it up again, letting it go, bringing it back a hundred times or more until gradually you absorb the power and the energy of that word and it begins to translate itself in your spiritual system into solid bone and muscle which in turn strengthens your Christian character and brings you closer into the 'image of his Son'.

One of the best periods to meditate is immediately before you fall to sleep at night. The last important thoughts on your mind in the evening before you go to sleep remain in your subconscious throughout the night. The mind works in strange ways while we are asleep, so make it work for spiritual achievement by pouring into it the word of God.

If the devil keeps you awake at night by throwing into your mind all kinds of evil thoughts and suggestions, then there is a simple remedy. Start to meditate on a passage from God's word, and I guarantee that the devil will soon let you get to sleep, for you can be sure that he would rather see you asleep than meditating on the word of God.

Sometimes, when people begin to put into practice the art of meditation immediately prior to going to sleep, they find that they have some very disturbing dreams. This is due to the fact that the word of God infiltrating the subconscious mind breaks up the thought patterns of a lifetime and these are siphoned off from the subconscious through dreams. There is nothing to be afraid of in this, as it normally lasts for a few nights and hardly ever recurs as long as the practice of meditation is continued.

Some find when they meditate on certain parts of Scripture (especially the book of Psalms) that they begin to feel a change in their whole emotional outlook. This is due to the fact that when the psalmists wrote those passages they were passing through periods of intense emotion. Some laughed, others cried, some felt pain or even shame. Meditation on such passages therefore often enables us to enter into the emotional atmosphere of the psalmists and this in turn deepens our own sensitivity to the things of God.

Meditation works to bring Christ's mind into ours by helping us to think as he thinks, feel as he feels and act as he would act. It reconstructs our thought-life, transforms our emotions and strengthens our will. With Christ's mind in ours, thought, feeling and will move together to produce the image of God's Son in us.

Let's remind ourselves of the value of meditation by looking again at the basic rules:

*Be definite* about the thing you want from God. A common failing among Christians is vagueness in their mind concerning the things they want. One must know what one wants with clarity and conviction.

Re-inforce your aim with strong desire. What is clear to the mind must also be hot to the heart. Some see the right thing with needle sharpness but they are cold in their *attitude* towards it.

Select suitable portions of Scripture related to the thing described. The power of scriptural meditation lies in taking into the mind the *word of God.* Other forms of meditation that leave out God's word as a basic factor are not for us. To be like Christ we absorb the word and assimilate it into our spiritual digestive systems where it will work to produce a healthy likeness to Christ.

Remember that meditation is not just simply memorizing. The word of God must *linger* in the mind. It must lie there, almost forgotten, and then be brought back into the mind in a constant process of methodical activity.

Use the moments before falling to *sleep* for purposeful meditation. These moments immediately prior to sleep are of the utmost value, and the thoughts of Scripture dropped into the mind at this time remain there throughout the night, affecting the mental attitudes and transforming the mind.

Meditation has been described as the mainspring of Christianity. Keep it wound up and you will never get 'run down'.

# 8

# *The Christian Way of Treating Trouble*

'I can't understand it,' said Paul, 'just when everything seemed to be going fine this had to happen. Now I'm back where I started, and I don't feel I can take any more. It's one thing after another. I get so angry and upset when things keep going wrong. If God loves me why does he allow these things to happen?'

Paul had been listening to an address I had been giving in a summer camp meeting on the subject of praise, and as soon as I came down from the platform he grabbed me by the arm and pleaded, 'Please can I talk to you for a minute.' The minute turned out to be an hour in which he poured out a sad story of setbacks and difficulties which had brought him to the verge of despair.

An hour's counselling helped Paul to recover his spiritual poise, but like him there are multitudes of Christians who view the problems that crowd into their lives as unwelcome intruders which ought never to be allowed. When troubles come our way the natural response is to ask, 'Why Lord, is this happening to me?' If no immediate answer is obvious we tend to become peeved and petulant, which further complicates the problem.

## How to treat trouble

Becoming a Christian doesn't mean that we are automatically delivered from problems or that we will never have to face serious difficulties. Jesus said, 'In the world ye shall have tribulation: but be of good cheer; I have overcome the world' (John 16:33). We should never be surprised when troubles come, and if you are going through a long list of difficulties at this very moment and you are wondering how you can get out of it then you are on the wrong track. The natural reaction is to show dismay at the approach of trouble, and happiness when the troubles are about to move away. The Christian approach to trouble is, however, vastly different.

Listen to this challenging word from one of the writers in the New Testament.

'When all kinds of trials and temptations crowd into your lives, my brothers, don't resent them as intruders, but *welcome them as friends!* Realise that they come to test your faith and to produce in you the quality of endurance' (James 1:2-3 PHILLIPS). The first time I read that statement I must admit I thought it was a mistranslation, but the more I pondered it the more I realized it contained distilled wisdom. The Christian is to welcome his trials and temptations as he would welcome a long lost friend, and at the first approach he sings excitedly, for he knows that in God's hand all the setbacks will be turned into springboards and all the stumbling blocks will become stepping stones.

'Hold on a moment,' I hear you say. 'Are you really serious?' In fact I am in dead earnest, especially as I find that nine out of ten Christians fail to put into practice this Christian approach to trouble. Most rejoice when the troubles go. Few welcome them as friends.

## God's point of view

If we are to see our troubles and difficulties in a Christian perspective, then we must learn to look at life from God's point of view. One of the most fascinating translations of Scripture (to my mind at least) is that of J.B. Phillips who translates a phrase in Colossians 1:9 like this: 'We are asking God that *you may see things . . . from his point of view* by being given spiritual insight and understanding.' If at this moment we could suddenly be transported to the side of God's eternal throne, and see as he sees, it would doubtless change our whole outlook on life in one split second. Seeing the end from the beginning we would look at our difficulties in a different light, aware of how God allows them, in order to use them to our advantage and for his glory.

The apostle Paul discovered this secret in his life, and it was this that sustained and supported him on his perilous journeys in the ancient world. Writing to the Colossian church from a prison cell, incarcerated for the gospel's sake and isolated from the Christians he so loved, he nevertheless cried, '*I rejoice* in my sufferings' (Colossians 1:24 italics mine).

The early Christians lived this way too. Flung to the jaws of red-jowled beasts purely to make sport for those on a Roman holiday, they were mauled to death with a song of praise upon their lips. Historians in tracing the progress of Christianity in those early centuries after Christ are convinced that the Christian faith conquered paganism by the way that its converts responded to their troubles.

Coming a little closer to our own time, consider Richard Williams, the medical missionary to Patagonia. On the night before he died he entered in his journal words that must stand out as some of the most moving words in all history. Huddled in the hull of his little boat, dying of scurvy and starvation, he wrote, 'Should anything prevent my ever adding to this, let all my beloved ones at home rest assured that I was happy beyond all expression, the night I wrote these lines, and would not have exchanged situations with any man living.'

Despite the fact that many Christians respond otherwise, this should be the *normal* response to life's problems and is in fact the spirit which is destined to conquer and convince the world.

## Saints under process

Someone has said that a Christian is like a tea bag—he is not worth much until he has been through some hot water. It seems to be a fact of human nature that learning and growth, development and change, require a process, and so often the most important changes take place within the framework of struggle. The psalmist said, 'Before I was afflicted I went astray: but now I have kept thy word.... It is good for me that I have been afflicted; that I might learn thy statutes' (Psalm 119:67, 71).

I have talked to many Christians who have stumbled over the fact that God allows trouble to invade their lives, but once they see that God permits pressure for a purpose, then a new sense of meaning flows into their souls. In overcoming the impediments of life we complete ourselves. The world around us is like an emery stone on which we sharpen our souls, and in a universe unbalanced to some degree by sin a lesson emerges through our adversities that it is not so much what *happens* to us but what *we do* with it that matters.

Things that strike into our lives make us bitter or better, according to the way we respond. As a plane takes off against the rising wind, so there have been multitudes in every age who, strengthened by Christ, have risen above their adverse environment to a new version of God and his glory.

## God permits all things for a purpose

In the very beginning when sin tore at God's universe, he could have swept aside Satan with one sweep of his great arm. But he chose to allow Satan to continue knowing that his efforts would in the end be turned to God's greater glory, and the final analysis would show that God's wisdom proved more than a match for satanic ingenuity.

One thing is sure—if we find ourselves in a situation or environment which is hostile to us, and which after prayer is not removed, there are resources provided by a loving God which when absorbed into our being enable us to rise above the problem with a song of praise in our hearts, and a joy that knows no despair. The same God who allowed his Son to die in apparent failure on a cross, yet wrought from it the greatest victory the world has ever known, is in charge of our lives; and there is nothing that can successfully work against a child of God who is related to him by personal faith in his Son, the Lord Jesus Christ.

The Bible expresss this truth in words much more meaningful than mine. 'All things work together for good to them that love God, to them who are called according to his purpose' (Romans 8:28).

God allows setbacks and difficulties to occur in our lives for a very significant purpose, and a proper response to the problems of life can in fact determine the rate of progress in our Christian experience. What are some of the purposes God has in allowing difficulties and irritations to enter our lives?

## Difficulties develop sensitivity...

This is the point of 2 Corinthians 1:3-4, that as God

comforts us and leads us through our difficulties and problems we become more deeply sensitive to the needs of others and thereby better equipped to help them: 'What a wonderful God we have—he is the Father of our Lord Jesus Christ, the source of every mercy, and the one who so wonderfully comforts and strengthens us in our hardships and trials. And why does he do this? So that when others are troubled, needing our sympathy and encouragement, we can pass on to them this same help and comfort God has given us' (TLB).

If we shrink from the difficulties and seek to be free of irritations, we may sever ourselves from potential benefits. But if we respond with expectancy and an open heart and mind, we will then allow God to achieve his highest purpose in us. The more problems you face and overcome the more God can use you in helping others know the deep meaning of his purpose for their lives.

## ...Deepen inward qualities...

We have already referred to Romans 8:28 in which we saw that God works all things to good in our lives, but the following verse in that chapter makes clear the underlying purpose for God's permitting trouble to enter our lives. 'For whom he did foreknow, he also did predestinate to be conformed to the image of his Son'.

Conformed to the image of his Son! This then is God's plan in allowing trouble to overtake us—he uses it to chisel and carve within us a likeness to his Son. With consummate artistry and skill he takes our trials as a diamond cutter would take his hardest stone, and presses it against the rough edges, shaping each facet to reflect the greatest light.

God's highest purpose for our lives is not simply to make us missionaries, preachers, evangelists, or teachers, but to make us like Christ. The pressures of trials and difficulties become in his hand a file by which he shapes within us the unmatched moral excellencies, the exquisite graces, the rare qualities of heart which reveal the image of his Son.

## ...And expand our world of opportunity

Trials and difficulties not only deepen our sympathy but expand our area of service. Christian biography is full of accounts of men and women who have transmuted their problems and transformed their irritations to make for more effective service. One thinks of Edward Irving lying prostrate with grief before the coffin of his dear dead son, then rising up to go to help others in similar distress. One thinks also of Josephine Butler standing before the balcony from which she watched her daughter plunge to her death, then after the funeral dedicating her whole life to the rescue of 'fallen women'. A hundred names spring to mind to testify that trouble can be transformed and lead to more determined and meaningful patterns of service.

We have seen something of God's purposes in allowing trials to overtake us. How then should we respond to this divine design?

Some rebel against it and become angry and bitter, impugning the justice of an almighty God. Nothing of course is more natural, but it is not the Christian way. Other just resign themselves to it, and shrug their shoulders saying, 'What is to be will be.' But the Christian does neither. He rejoices in it, treating his troubles as opportunities to draw closer to God, deepen his character and advance his service. He does not resign himself with a sullen 'Amen' but rejoices in it with a triumphant 'Hallelujah!'.

We meet our troubles head on with praise, welcoming

them (as the Scripture says) as friends. If we respond incorrectly to our problems we may allow anger to overtake us, and one of the secrets of a life free from anger is to *receive all trials and temptations with praise.* Praising God for the problem enables us to keep our whole being open to God, so that he can use the trial or difficulty in just the way he wants to for our greater benefit.

If we ignore the Scripture's advice and respond to our problems with irritation, dismay and despair, we will allow a root of bitterness to spread inside us that will threaten our whole spiritual welfare. 'Be careful,' writes the author of the epistle to the Hebrews, 'that none of you fails to respond to the grace which God gives, for if he does there can very easily spring up in him a bitter spirit which is not only bad in itself but can also poison the lives of many others' (Hebrews 12:15 PHILLIPS).

We are what we respond to, nothing more nothing less. Every moment of our lives we are responding to either the problem or the grace that God provides.

## God's obligation

You see, God has committed himself to supplying a special stream of grace for every Christian, and has promised that 'no temptation has come your way that is too hard for flesh and blood to bear. But God can be trusted not to allow you to suffer any temptation beyond your powers of endurance. He will see to it that every temptation has its way out, so that it will be possible for you to bear it' (1 Corinthians 10:13 PHILLIPS). To his servant Paul he said, 'My grace is enough for you: for where there is weakness, my power is shown the more completely' (2 Corinthians 12:9 PHILLIPS).

When a trial or temptation comes you turn in one of two directions—towards the problem or towards the grace which God provides. Turning to the problem produces anger, irritability and sometimes depression, but turning towards the grace that God provides enables you to become creatively objective, so that you rise above the difficulty and touch God in a new and vibrant way.

So when problems or trials and difficulties crowd into my life, what should I do?

I will meet them head on with praise. Recognizing that I belong to God and I am his personal responsibility, I know he would never allow anything to happen to me that could not be turned to my ultimate good. While praising him for the problems, however, I will not allow myself to become insensitive to any deficiencies in me which may have caused the problem, and will seek to examine my life at every single opportunity.

I will ask myself, did I cause this problem by something I failed to do? If I did, then I will correct the fault at once and will praise God even further that the problem has enabled me to add something to my inward character.

As I praise God I know that no anger can invade my spirit. No bitterness can sear my soul. Without haughtiness, or pride, I can say from the depth of my heart, God loves me. I am the crown of his creation: he put me together in eternity and knew every detail of my being before I was ever born.

Knowing me as he does, he has a plan for my life that cannot be frustrated. He will allow nothing to happen to me that will not contribute to his glory and my good. I will respond to his love and grace with all the enthusiasm I can muster.

In this thrilling revelation I will continually rejoice, and be glad.

Praise the Lord!

# 9

# *Building the Bridge of Prayer*

'But I find prayer so boring. When I get down on my knees my mind goes blank and I just don't know what to say. Isn't there some kind of system Christians use when they pray? Can you help me to overcome this difficulty I have in relation to prayer?'

The speaker was a young student by the name of Jim who had recently made a commitment to Christ while at college and had come for counselling on the subject of prayer. After his conversion he felt instinctively that he ought to pray, but whenever he got down on his knees and tried to talk with God his mind went blank, with the result that he had become extremely frustrated over the whole question of prayer.

I explained that our rate of progress in the Christian life is determined by how much time we give to prayer and went on to provide him with a simple pattern on which he could build a meaningful prayer relationship with the Lord Jesus Christ. By now I am sure the scaffolding I gave him has dropped away and he has built for himself a strong structure of prayer through which he can express his own individuality, but the steps he took helped him so much I feel constrained to include them here.

Prayer is one of the most vital aspects of the Christian life. No one who scamps the practice of prayer will ever know the transforming power of Christ's personality upon his own, as intimacy with the Master comes only in relation to the time given, day by day, to the *continued* practice of prayer.

Prayer quite simply is a conversation with God, and as all conversation involves *listening* as well as talking no one can become expert in the art of prayer until they learn to listen as well as to speak. In fact some teachers on the subject of prayer suggest that a good way to measure our effectiveness or progress in this matter is to ask ourselves whether we would rather hear God speak than to listen to ourselves speak. The honest answer to that question will indicate just how much we have progressed since first we started to pray.

Every Christian needs some kind of pattern on which to build a life of prayer and when this is followed it leads to success in what must be considered as one of the most important areas of Christian experience.

## Begin each day with God

As soon as you awake in the morning turn your thoughts instantly to Christ, and the moment sleep leaves your eyes centre your mind fully upon him. You will be tempted of course to let your mind wander to other things, but the more you learn to salute your Master in these opening moments of the day, the more meaningful the whole of your day will become.

We have already spoken of the blessings of meditation, so let the same word that rested on your mind the night before be there now to engage your attention as you awake. Think on his word, and as you do, lift your heart in praise to God to thank him for the blessing of sleep, the refreshment of the night and the challenge of a new day.

Remember this is going to be the first day of the rest of

your life. You have never seen it before and you will never see it again. Rich possibilities open up before you, so greet the morning with praise. Whatever the weather outside, receive everything with gratitude and learn to rejoice in both the sunshine and the storm. Think on the royal relationship that you have with heaven. God is your Father, Jesus is your Saviour, the Holy Spirit is your Comforter, the word of God is your Guide, the angels assist in your protection and all things will work together for good because you love God.

Isn't that enough to be glad about?

## Fence off part of the day

As soon as possible after the day has commenced get alone with God for a time of personal prayer. It may not always be possible upon rising from bed, but watch that before the day gets too busy you have taken time to spend some minutes with your Lord in prayer. The time of this morning devotion will vary from one person to another, but it ought to be at least fifteen minutes.

Andrew Murray recalls asking a gathering of Christians in a large convention how many spent thirty minutes a day in prayer. One hand went up. How many spent fifteen minutes a day? Not half the hands were raised. How many spent five minutes a day? All the hands went up, but afterwards, at least one said he did not know whether he spent even five minutes a day in prayer.

The age in which we live is so fast moving that many Christians make the excuse that they have little time to pray. It has been said that if we are too busy to pray then we are busier than God intended us to be. Prayer is worth more than all the time it takes.

Tagore once told this parable. 'I had gone a-begging from door to door in the village path when a golden chariot appeared in the distance and I wondered if this was the King of Kings! The chariot stopped where I stood. The master's glance fell on me. Suddenley the master held out his hand and said, 'What have you got to give me?' I was stunned. A King opening his hand to a beggar. I was confused but slowly from my wallet I took out the least little grain of corn and gave it to him. How great my surprise when at the end of the day I emptied my bag on the floor, and there I found a little grain of gold among the poor heap. I wept bitterly and wished I had the heart to have given all to him.'

If we give God one moment he will turn it into gold, but if we give him an hour—what then? As you learn to love prayer you will crave more time for it. No time will be too much time. What moments you give to him will come back a thousandfold.

Rosemary, a member of the Worldwide Chain of Prayer for Revival, wrote asking what advice I could give her on the question of prayer. Her letter was full of hints that she had little time and it would be hopeless me saying that she should do as John Wesley did and give at least two to three hours a day to God in personal prayer. I gave her the advice I am giving you—start with fifteen minutes and see what happens.

She did, and weeks later wrote back a breezy letter saying how wonderful her days were now that she gave God fifteen minutes every morning. 'The day stands out bold, and clear,' she wrote, 'after I have prayed. Before I used to wonder what to do next, but . . . it is so different.'

My next letter carried the suggestion, 'If God can do so much with fifteen minutes, just think what he could do with an hour!' I did not hear from her for several weeks, as she had been experimenting with her new programme of prayer. At last her letter came.

'There are no words to explain what God is doing in my

life. The more time I give to him the more time I seem to have to myself. I don't know how he does it. All I know is, he does.'

## Carefully select Scripture

A few verses of Scripture reverently read will help prime the pump of your spirit so that you can come before the Lord with an open heart. Those who use devotional aids, such as *Every Day with Jesus* or *Scripture Union Notes* will find that the thoughts contained in these readings will help flood the mind with spiritual meaning and open the whole being to the Lord.

Many (I have found) fail to get the best out of such daily devotionals because they dismiss too quickly from their minds the thoughts contained in them. Once you have read the relative Scripture, and pursued the thought for the day, don't just dismiss it and move to something else, but *ponder it.* Reflect on what you read. Ask God to help you squeeze out of his word every single ounce of blessing. Meditate for a moment on the significance of the thoughts contained both in the text and in the devotional thought, until you feel sure that there is nothing more you can extract from it.

Those who do not use daily devotional aids will need to select their morning reading carefully. Don't just let the Bible drop open, but have some kind of a planned reading so that you move through the word of God with a definite aim. There are many different kinds of study aids and any Christian bookshop will help you with information on this matter.

## Follow with praise

The psalmist declared, 'I will praise the Lord no matter

what happens. I will constantly speak of his glories and grace' (Psalm 34:1 TLB). The question is sometimes raised by some Christians—can I really be expected to praise the Lord at all times? Surely it means *most* times, or *some* times. One cannot be expected to praise the Lord when the days are dark and dreary?

Not so, says the psalmist. He will praise the Lord 'at all times'. However dark the day may appear to be, take the advice of the psalmist and enter into God's presence with praise.

Think on the wonder of a sinner such as you finding a welcome in the presence of a most Holy God and being allowed to linger before his throne of grace. Rejoice in the knowledge that God owns the world and has everything under control. No exploding bombs can blast the pillars of his eternal throne. Even in the darkest hours there is always something to be thankful for, so as you come before him, think on these things and let your heart swell with gratitude and thanksgiving rise.

## Make a daily commitment

As you are already a committed Christian it does not mean that you have to repeat that commitment day by day, but you will be well advised to remind yourself that without him you can do nothing, and that your success, your ability, your strength comes directly from the Lord. Look ahead into the day with your Lord and remember that you and he are partners. You may find yourself praying like this. 'We have a full day together Lord, and there is so much to be done.' Step by step cover the day in advance as you picture yourself in a dozen different situations—yet always in company with your Lord.

Perhaps there is a difficult letter to write. You will need special guidance for that. Or an especially delicate matter to raise with someone for which you will need more than natural wisdom. Though most things are known to you, remember *everything* is known to him and he see the end of that day from the beginning in one panoramic vision. You need him to be with you every step of the way, so recognize this and daily surrender your whole being into his hands.

## Personal intercession

Praying for the needs of others should be a regular part of our prayer time. Many I know keep a list of prayer requests, but his must be watched very carefully as it is possible to build up a list of items that should not really be there at all. Don't add names just for the sake of adding them, but be convinced with each one that there is something in which God wants *you* to share.

An important matter may be brought to your attention over which you may feel some concern, but before you add it your list of regular prayer, pause for a few moments and seek to feel the witness of the Holy Spirit whether this should become a part of your daily prayer pattern. It may be that God wants someone else to intercede over that matter and that he has a different need in which he wants you to participate. Effective prayer depends so much on discovering which way God is moving—then move with him.

You prayer list will change from week to week. Some things of course will stay for weeks, months and perhaps years, such as the needs of your local church, your home, unsaved loved ones, etc.. Don't get into bondage over a prayer list, however, or think that every time you hear of a need it has to be added to your programme. Bear in mind also that sometimes God will lay upon your heart a special burden which may not even be on your list (and need not even be added) as it will be but the passing movement of the Spirit that will last for a few moments of intercessory prayer and then be lifted. This the way God works, laying a burden for a few moments, upon one, and then another, moving through the body of Christ to use its members in united compassion.

Personal petition should be kept to the last. In this way you will guard against selfishness in prayer. Unless we are careful egocentricity can rear its head even in the prayer closet, but when we keep our own personal prayer petitions to the last we eliminate the possibility of building our prayer concern just around ourselves.

## Let God talk to you

We saw at the beginning that prayer is basically a two-way conversation. The cultivation of the listening side of prayer is best seen (in my opinion) in Mrs Herman's book entitled *Creative Prayer.*

'The alert and courageous soul making its first venture upon the spiritual life is like a wireless operator on his trial trip in the Pacific. At the mercy of a myriad electrical whispers the novice does not know what to think. How fascinating are those ghostly pipings and mutterings, delicate scratchings and thin murmers—and how confusing. Now he catches the plaintive mummerings of a P & O liner trying to reach a French steamer; now the silvery tinkle from a Japanese gunboat seeking its shore station. There are aimless but curiously insistent noises, like grains of sand tumbling across tar paper; these are the so called "static" noises of the atmosphere adjusting itself to a state of electrical balance. Now the operator thinks he has got his message, but it is only the murmured greeting of ships that pass in the night.

'And then just as his ear has begun to get adjusted to the

weird babel of crossing sounds there comes a remote and thrilling whisper that plucks at his taut nerves and makes him forget all his newly acquired knowledge. It is the singing of the spheres, the electrical turmoil of stars beyond the reach of the telescope, the birth cry and death wail of worlds. Suddenly there comes a squeaking nervous spark, sharp as the squeal of a frightened rat. He decides to ignore it, and then suddenly realises that it is calling the name of his own boat. It is the unexpected message and *he nearly missed it.'*

As we wait before God and learn as a wireless operator does to disentangle the ghostly whisperings from the real message, then prayer becomes a thrilling adventure. Through the daily practice of prayer and communion with God the soul develops a sensitivity to the Holy Spirit and soon learns to distinguish between the voice of the subconscious, the world, personal ambition, self-will, unbridled imagination, and the voice of God. One Christian writer claims that one such hour of listening can give us a deeper insight into the mysteries of God's will than a year's hard study in theology.

This covers of course the subject of early morning prayer and the need to build an effective pattern on which to build a daily devotion, but there will be other times during the day when you will need to get alone with God and pray through some special problem which requires even more intensive prayer. In Christian circles when prayer is made on behalf of others it is usually termed intercession; when made on behalf of oneself it is called petition.

The ministry of intercession is without doubt one of the greatest ministries of the Christian life. There is no human glory given to intercessors, for they work in secret and their service is known (in most cases) only to God. The preacher may have his admiring audience, and the evangelist his fame, but the intercessor receives no human admiration or applause.

## Fasting has value

But all those who come before God in deep intensive intercession or petition should know of the added value and power that comes to prayer through the spiritual fast. Those whom God has used greatly in Christian service have recognized the importance of reinforcing prayer in this way. Fasting means abstaining from eating. Common in Christ's day, it was in fact a part of Christ's own ministry, and continued in the early church (see Mark 2:18-20; Acts 27:9).

It is not possible to go into all the aspects of the spiritual fast in this book, but there are some excellent volumes on this subject which lay down guidelines for those who wish to know more of this important aspect of Christian teaching.

## At the close of day

So much for the daytime, but what should happen at the close of the day, when the evening closes in and it is time to retire? We have already emphasized the importance of meditation before we enter into sleep, but before this you need to spend at least ten minutes with the Lord in quiet prayer.

It is desirable to review the whole of the day in God's presence and to look back over the various situations, pausing to ask for forgiveness or confessing any wrongs that may have been committed. Don't go to sleep until the day has been reviewed in the light of God. You will sleep better when your penitence is blessed by his pardon.

There will be cause for praise and thanksgiving too—

where God's promises have been seen to be fulfilled. Remember the mind continues to work in strange ways even when we are asleep. Let it work—put it to work on the best things. Thoughts of peace hold the mind in the hours of resting and are by far the best sedative. This also provides a tone for the day that lies ahead.

Some may see no need for a prayer pattern, preferring to leave prayer to the feeling of the hour or the mood of the moment. We can vary the pattern of course as God appoints. A pattern is not like a cake that is spoilt if one ingredient is left out.

But the best way to learn the art of prayer is to pray!

# 10

# *Meeting and Mastering Temptation*

'I haven't long returned from the most wonderful Christian youth camp I have ever attended, but since I have been home it seems all hell has been let loose. God met me in a wonderful way at the camp and I thought, after that, temptation wouldn't worry me any more. Now it seems I am tempted more than I was before. Is there something wrong with my experience?' A young man by the name of Barry had come for counselling because of the difficulties he was facing with the subject of temptation. As I encouraged him to share with me some further details, he went on: 'When I was at the camp, one night the Lord ministered to me in such a way that I felt I was walking on air. For days afterwards I felt as if I could have stood up to the devil face to face, and even now I feel the glow of that experience deep within me, but the trouble is, though the Lord seems more real than ever before, temptation has become equally more real. I used to be tempted a great deal with wrong thoughts, and things like that, but now the temptations come so fast and furious I wonder whether I am going to be able to cope. Can you help me?'

I couldn't help but feel a great deal of sympathy for Barry, because he was coming face to face with a principle which many people encounter in their Christian experience but fail to understand. And that principle is this—God does not allow temptation to come our way in order to destroy what he has given, but to deepen it. Barry seemed an eager listener, so I shared with him that day some of the more salient biblical facts regarding temptation, and after about an hour together he seemed to be greatly relieved. As the whole subject of temptation and how to meet it and master it is of paramount importance in Christian living, let me try and put into focus for you the truths I shared with Barry that day.

## Temptation has a purpose

Temptation has its uses. As we grapple, we grow. But before we can really understand the reason why God allows temptation, and how he uses it to deepen and develop our lives, we must first recognize the fact that *God does not tempt.* Listen to what one New Testaments writer says on this subject:

> And remember, when someone wants to do wrong it is never God who is tempting him, for God never wants to do wrong and never tempts anyone else to do it. Temptation is the pull of man's own evil thoughts and wishes. These evil thoughts lead to evil actions and afterwards to the death penalty from God. So don't be misled, dear brothers. [James 1:13-16 TLB.]

But although God does not tempt he can (and often does) lead us to the place of temptation. When Jesus was anointed by the Holy Spirit at his baptism in the river Jordan, the Scripture says that Jesus was 'led up of the Spirit into the wilderness to be tempted of the devil' (Matthew 4:1). When we examine Luke's account of the temptation we find an intriguing thought, as he says, 'And Jesus being full of the Holy Ghost returned from Jordan, and was led by the Spirit into the wilderness' (Luke 4:1).

Later, in verse 14, it says that 'Jesus returned in the power of the Spirit of Galilee'. When Jesus went into temptation he went in '*full* of the Spirit'. When he came out it was 'in the *power* of the Spirit'. In the life of Jesus all that temptation could achieve was to turn fullness into power.

Dr G Campbell Morgan, in his book *The Crises of the Christ,* claims that we ought to make a clear distinction between the two words 'fullness' and 'power'. The 'fullness of the Spirit', he argues, 'is what happens when the Spirit is bestowed upon us; the "power" of the Spirit is what happens when that fullness is tested through the process of temptation.' Here we begin to get a glimpse of the deep underlying purpose as to why God allows us to be tempted—it is a testing ground by which we can turn fullness into power. Those who seek to follow in the footsteps of the Lord Jesus Christ must learn that the power of the Spirit is never realized save through some wilderness of personal conflict with our adversary, the devil. Some enter into the wilderness in the fullness of the Spirit and come out broken and incapable of further service. Others go in with fullness and come out with the tread and force of conscious power.

## A right attitude to temptation

What is it that makes the difference between defeat and victory in relation to the subject of temptation? It hinges on our attitude towards temptation. If we face the wilderness in the spirit of complacency, then the devil is invariably the victor. If we face it in the spirit of complete dependence upon the Lord, and with a determination to do his will, then we come out with the thrilling consciousness that power tested becomes power that is triumphant. As far as Christ was concerned, the assailing winds of temptation served only to strengthen him and bring him forth in the power of the Spirit. Moffat's translation of the moment when Jesus rebutted Satan's temptation in the wilderness, as recorded in Matthew 4:10-11, reads: 'Begone, Satan! it is written, You must worship the Lord your God, and serve him *alone!* At this the devil left him' (italics mine). The way Moffat translates this passage seems to suggest that when Jesus used the word 'alone' the devil left him. One commentator says of this translation of Moffat's, 'Satan could not stand that word "alone" and when Jesus uttered it, he turned and left because he knew that to tempt a man who stands on that word "alone" in a single-minded allegiance to God is only to strengthen that man and deepen rather than destroy his confidence in the Almighty.'

The apostle Paul presented the same truth in these words, when he said, ' "All things are good for me?" Yes, but I am not going to let anything master me' (1 Corinthians 6:12 Moffat). The reason why Paul couldn't be mastered by anything was because he was mastered by God, and unless we are mastered by God then we will soon be mastered by *things*—temptation included. Because Jesus was so completely surrendered to the will and purpose of God, the forces of temptation served only to strengthen him. When we follow in our Master's footsteps and stand on God *alone,* then the evil one plays a losing game because all he succeeds in doing is strengthening us through his temptations, enabling us to come out on the victory side in everything.

One thing becomes crystal clear as we examine the temptation of our Lord Jesus Christ—temptation should not just be borne; it should be used. The secret of using temptation and turning it to our advantage is one of life's greatest secrets. Once we have learned it, we are unbeatable and unbreakable. A Christian schoolteacher told me some time ago of a remark made by a child in her class whey they were discussing the subject of Christ's death on the cross. The teacher had said, 'Jesus was called upon to bear his cross, just as we are called upon to bear our cross. At that point, one little girl had interrupted and said, 'Miss, Jesus didn't bear his cross—he used it.' Out of the mouths of babes and sucklings!

When we view temptation with the right attitude, and face it with the strength God gives, then the very opposition we face becomes a spur. The Russians have a saying that goes like this: 'The same hammer that shatters glass, forges steel.' The truth is, there is no temptation, trial, difficulty or opposition ever designed by Satan that cannot be taken and used for higher ends. Everything, even temptation, can enrich us if we know how to handle it and make it work towards positive ends. Philosophers have told us repeatedly that life is determined more by reactions than by actions. Temptation may sweep in upon us, or force its way into our lives, without our asking and sometimes without our acting, and it is at such moments that our reactions play an important part. We can react with self-pity or frustration, or we can act with confidence and courage, making the temptation work to improve our character and deepen our hold upon God. The temptation when it comes may contain an evil design, but by the time we have finished with it, providing we respond correctly, the evil has been turned into good.

Some years ago when I was in Nairobi, Kenya, I preached at a service which was conducted in the Swahili language. They sang a song, the tune of which I instantly recognized as 'Lord, we are able'. I whispered to the minister in charge of the service, 'What are the words of this hymn?' He thought for a moment and said, 'Lord, we can take it'. I smiled to myself and I remember thinking, 'That's it—we can take anything that comes, for we can use it to divine ends.' When temptation bears down upon us, providing we respond correctly, then all it can do is plough the field in which we sow and reap God's harvest.

## Why does God allow temptation?

The question is often asked, especially by young Christians, 'Why does God allow temptation?' In order to answer that question correctly, we must pause for a moment to look at the meaning of the Greek word for temptation, *peirasmos.* It means to test, to try, or to prove. The biblical use of the word, unlike the modern use of it, does not contain the thought of seduction or entrapment, but rather the putting of a person to a test for the purpose of deepening personal qualities. This then is the purpose behind temptation—it is God's way of helping us to deepen inward qualities and develop our character. Dr Oswald Chambers says, 'God can, in one single moment, make a heart pure, but not even God himself can give a person *character.*' It is essential that we are subjected to testing, for character would not be the precious thing it is if it could be acquired without effort, without combat and without contradictions. 'Virtue that has not been tried,' said one great theologian, 'does not deserve the name of virtue.'

This now raises the question: what is character? Someone has described it in this way: 'Character is what we are in the dark.' Character is different from reputation. Reputation is what other people think of us; character is what we are on the inside. To many people the thought of God allowing his children to be tested is inconsistent with his omnipotence. 'If God is almighty,' they reason, 'then he should intervene in the devil's attempts to seduce the children of God and prevent him from having access to their personalities.' However, it is precisely *because* God is omnipotent that he allows his children to be tempted. F.P. Harton in arguing this point says, 'A conquering nation, that is not sure of its own strength, refuses to allow the people it subjects any kind of independence at all and keeps control with a strong hand—but the real motive is fear.' Well, God does not control his universe through fear, but by love, power and eternal justice. Although he allows his children to be tempted for the express purpose of building character, he ensures that to each one there flows a stream of grace, which, if received, enables them to overcome the temptation and rise above it (see 1 Corinthians 10:13). One of the devil's devices, in attacking God's children, is to attempt to persuade them that God is not able to help them in the time of temptation. But God is well able to help them and does so, not always by delivering them from it but by giving them his grace to overcome it.

## Temptation develops our prayer life

But not only does God allow temptation in order to help us develop character, he allows it also to develop greater prowess in prayer. New Zealand, I am told, has no dangerous animals and no dangerous reptiles native to it. It is also the home of more flightless birds than any other country in the world—the kiwi, the kakapo, the penguin and the weka rail. Scholars believe there is a close connection between these two facts. As food was always abundant—and there was no danger near—no fearsome beast or reptile, the birds have no necessity to spread their wings and fly. With no necessity to fly they soon lost their ability to fly. No necessity—no ability. Is it not the same in human life? The very temptation we dread compels us to expand the wings of the spirit and drives us towards the throne of God in prayer. Do we not pray most when we feel we need most? If there was no temptation, no fierce pressure from the evil one, then perhaps we might not use the wings of prayer as much, and our appearances before the thone of grace might be few and far between. Martin Luther claimed that his temptations were his 'Masters of Divinity' which taught him more about prayer than all his formal training as a priest.

## Ways to meet temptation

Now we have some idea of what temptation is and why God allows it, we must give our attention to ways by which we can meet it and master it. The first way is what we are going to call the way of *prevention*. Some of the best defences we make against temptation are those we make ahead of time. This is why the words of Jesus, 'Watch and pray, that you enter not into temptation' which he uttered prior to his ordeal at Calvary, stand out in deep and bold significance. The deeper our prayer life prior to temptation, the more effective will be our ability to cope with it when it comes.

What I am saying here should not be seen as a contradiction of what I said earlier, that temptation serves to deepen one's prayer life. Some might be saying to themselves at this stage: 'If temptation serves to deepen prayer, then what is the point of preparing to meet temptation by prayer—the argument seems to be circular.'

Let's see if we can reconcile the two paradoxical statements. No amount of preventive praying will eliminate moments of temptation, but it will help us to build strong spiritual defences so that when temptation comes we are not engulfed by it. We will still need to pray when temptation comes, but the prayer we have put in beforehand will stand us in good stead when confronted by strong and fierce temptation.

We must try to begin every day with prayer, for the climate that develops in our souls through the time we spend in prayer will be the climate in which we live out the day that lies ahead of us. 'I pray everywhere,' some Christians say, 'at all times, and thus I have no need to pray at specific times.' My experience has been different. I find if I do not pray at specific times them I am not inclined to pray at any time. The 'everywhere' is sustained only by a 'somewhere' and the 'all times' by a 'specific time'. so look into the face of God every morning, through personal communion, then rise from your prayer time to project the prayer climate into the rest of your day.

Another way we can develop resistance to meet temptation and thus prepare ourselves in advance (the way of prevention) is by gaining a *working knowledge of the Bible.* This is why Jesus was so successful in his rebuttal of Satan in the wilderness. When the devil said, 'It is written . . . Jesus replied, 'It is written *again.'* The devil knew how to use certain texts to his advantage, but he was no match for Jesus, who knew and understood the entire scope of the Old Testament scriptures. If we are to be successful in meeting and mastering temptation we must do more than fill our minds with a few Bible texts—*we must seek to understand and grasp the Bible as a whole.* Storing up key texts in our minds for use in times of trial and difficulty is good and extremely valuable, but it does not take the place of a systematic and methodical study of the Scriptures.

We saw a few moments ago how the devil tried to use a text to his advantage, but it was a text taken out of its context—and all that succeeds in becoming is a pretext. If you examine carefully the record of Christ's temptation in the wilderness you will find that the devil approached Christ on three levels, to which our Lord used three separate scriptures as a form of rebuttal. The order in which Satan levelled his temptations was thus—bread, trust, worship. This is typical of Satan's approach to the human heart—I will give you bread if you give me your trust and then your worship. This the exact opposite to the order in which these three texts appear in the Scriptures in Deuteronomy—8:3; 6:16 and 6:13. God's order is there laid down as, first worship, secondly trust, and thirdly bread. God says, 'Give me your worship, and your trust and then bread will follow.' Put in another form it would read, 'Seek ye first the kingdom of God, and his righteousness; and all these things shall be added unto you' (Matthew 6:33). Although the devil knew how to use texts, Jesus knew how to use the Bible. To build effective barriers against temptation, seek to understand and comprehend not just sections of the Bible but the whole of it.

Another way of taking preventive measures against the forces of temptation is to ensure that one is *filled with the Spirit.* Without going into the theological implications of the phrase 'filled with the Spirit' we must all surely agree that Christians experience, apart from the power and plentitude of the Spirit, is utterly ineffective and unproductive. F.W. Boreham in one of his delightful books tells of a town in Australia where the officials arranged the digging of a five-mile canal as a means of joining one river to another. Not long after the canal was finished and water began to run through it, there appeared in its waters some evil-smelling and highly obnoxious weeds. The foul smell the weeds gave off caused a good deal of discomfort and anxiety to those who lived along the banks. Many remedies were tried—all without success. Then one day someone came up with a bright idea—willow trees. They planted the trees along the banks of the canal and within six months the offending weeds had dried and disappeared. What had happened? In some strange way the willow trees had siphoned out of the water the very chemicals which the weeds needed if they were to survive, and so, cut off from their sustaining force they just shrivelled up and died.

This story comes home with all the force of a biblical parable, for it is only as we live out our lives in the power of the Spirit that the weeds of our carnal nature become starved of nourishment and, like the weeds in the canal, shrivel up and die.

Some Christians believe that at conversion the Holy Spirit comes in to fill the newly converted personality and then one needs daily to appropriate what the Holy Spirit has deposited there potentially. If that is your belief then make sure that you are opening you life day by day and hour by hour to the presence and power of the Holy Spirit who is resident within. My own view concerning the ministry of the Holy Spirit in the life of a believer is that, although the Holy Spirit does come in at conversion, there is available a subsequent experience of the Spirit whereby he comes 'upon' a believer to empower, strengthen and equip for service. Whatever theological view you take concerning the operation and ministry of the Holy Spirit in your life, one thing is clear: we need continually and continuously to expose our beings to the flow of the Spirit so that he might work in us his will and purpose.

Last but not least of the preventive measures which should be taken against the force of temptation is to *remove from your life the things that might contribute to defeat.* Paul's advice to the Christians in Rome was this: 'Put ye on the Lord Jesus Christ, and make not provision for the flesh, to fulfil the lusts thereof' (Romans 13:14). Examine your life to see if there are hidden provisions for defeat lying there—impure books, sensual pictures, letters, records, etc.. Only as we take steps to remove these things from our lives can we expect to find victory.

A young man once followed me to the vestry of a church where I had preached on the subject of temptation and confessed that for years he had been unable to cope with the lustful images that entered his mind. I suspected, when talking to him, that his problem would not be so long standing unless in some way it was being fed, and I discovered, after long questioning, that every night prior to going to sleep he spent ten or fifteen minutes poring over 'girlie' magazines. It never occurred to him that there was a connection between his nightly actions and the images he could not get out of his mind during the day, while in church, or when he tried to pray. I encouraged him to go home and destroy the magazines—which I am glad to say he did. When I talked to him months later he seemed to be extremely embarrassed. I probed him as to why he should feel embarrassed upon meeting me. This was his reply. 'The advice you gave me to remove out of my life the things that were contributing to my defeat was so simple, but so effective, I felt so foolish for not having seen it myself. Since I acted on your advice my thought life has been transformed.'

## Flight—better than fight

You might think from what I have been saying in this chapter that the only correct response to temptation is to square up to it and confront it. This is not always true, however, for there are some occasions when it is better to run from temptation than to stay and try to fight it.

In 2 Timothy 2:22 Paul gives Timothy this advice. 'Run from anything that gives you the evil thoughts that young men often have, but stay close to anything that makes you want to do right' (TLB). A young man who experienced great difficulty in his thought life after passing a cinema, on his way to and from work, which displayed nude photographs, thought that the answer to his problem was to be found in persisting to pass the cinema until the nude photographs no longer bothered him. When he confided to a friend his problem, he was advised to take another route to and from his work, and when he did this the problem in his thought life cleared up of its own accord. It ought to be kept in mind that on certain occasions flight is better than fight.

## The way of circumvention

Now that we have examined several ways by which we can prepare ourselves to meet temptation—the way of prevention—we now need to consider some of the ways by which we can handle temptation when it comes. This is what I like to call the way of circumvention. What, if after all our efforts to prepare ourselves for temptation, it still strikes with paralysing force? How do we handle it?

*First.* When temptation strikes you (an evil thought, a wrong sexual impulse, etc) stop whatever you are doing and concentrate on something else. A man I know tells of how one day when walking through a field he was overtaken by an evil thought. He deliberately picked up a heavy log and struggled with it back home. He said that the attention he needed to give to carry the heavy log made him forget the evil thought. The principle behind this action is to take on yourself a task heavy enough and demanding enough to occupy your whole attention. The greatest temptations come not when you are absorbed in a task but when you are idle or when nothing particularly absorbs you.

*Secondly.* Another way you can meet and master temptation is this—if you are alone when an evil thought enters your mind, deliberately go, if possible, to a group of people. Being with a group (especially if it is a Christian group) tends to draw the mind to other interests. We sometimes talk of the temptations of crowds, but there are times when being with people can help us from harbouring thoughts that are poisonous and injurious to our souls.

*Thirdly.* Change any wrong mental picture that enters

your mind into a spiritual one. Evil thoughts are not driven out by dwelling upon them, even guiltily or prayerfully. The longer they stay in the focus of attention the deeper they are burned on the memory and the more mental associations they produce. They must be outwitted by swiftly directing the mind to some other absorbing theme. Train your mind to run at once to thoughts of your crucified Lord. To think of him is to summon him to your aid. It is not difficult to understand the simple psychology of this approach, for Christ is the centre of all things pure. The thought that looked so seductive a moment before, looks loathsome when Jesus is present.

*Fourthly.* Train your eyes to see only what you want them to see. One of the most righteous men who ever lived was Job. A key to his righteousness is found in Job 31:1—'I made a covenant with mine eyes; why then should I think upon a maid?' The key to controlling the mind is to control the eyes. But what sort of agreement should we make with our eyes? We should purpose to look only at those things which God approves. One man I heard of, who was often overcome with lustful thoughts when looking at members of the opposite sex, said, 'I trained myself to look not at a woman's body, but at her face.' It helped him, he said, to conquer the battle that had been going on in his mind, and the covenant he made with his eyes helped him overcome a problem that, in the past, he had not been able to win.

*Fifthly.* Strengthen your will by a bond of accountability. This is one of the most powerful principles you can learn in relation to meeting and mastering temptation. Whenever we tell ourselves we are going to do something, then we have only ourselves to answer to, but if we tell someone else what we are going to do we double our accountability. So make a covenant with a close friend, a marriage partner, a youth leader, a minister, that when you next meet a temptation that you find difficult to handle you will contact that person and share it with them for united prayer. If you do this three things will happen: (1) the thought of having to share your problem with another person will, in itself, be a powerful motivation to resist the temptation; (2) when you tell the other person the facts concerning your problem and temptation, that will motivate the other person to provide a spiritual umbrella for you, and thus contribute to his or her own spirituality; (3) the other person's prayers alongside your own will provide a powerful force for victory. A Christian husband I know, who was often overcome with impure thoughts, shared this fact with his wife and asked her, whenever she saw him taking a long look at another woman, to accept that as a signal that she should say something about that woman which would help him to see her from God's point of view. She would say something like, 'Isn't it wonderful to know that Jesus died on the cross for that woman?' The man found through the co-operation of his wife a victory over his thought-life he never dreamed was possible.

*Sixthly.* Purpose to curb your curiosity. Undisciplined curiosity is one of the greatest reasons for defeat in our thought life. God has given us a marvellous intellect but, in the interests of our spiritual life, he has given us an important limitation—we are not to learn the details of evil through experimenting with it, but to recognize it with a sensitive and sanctified spirit. Paul when writing to the Romans said, 'I would have you wise unto that which is good, and simple concerning evil' (Romans 16:19). Adam and Eve were defeated in the garden of Eden due to the fact that they allowed their curiosity to push them beyond the boundaries God had set. In their pre-sinless state they were well equipped by God to detect evil in their spirits, but over-curiosity prompted them to experiment with the thought that had been presented to them by the serpent, and by such experimenting they entered into sin. In today's terms it means that we who are God's children should be extremely careful about our innate curiosity, and however curious we find ourselves becoming about such things as nudity, provocative plays on television, or sensual books, we must stop and remind ourselves that God expects us to put a limit on our curiosity and refrain from crossing the boundaries which take us into sin.

*Seventhly.* Use impure and evil thoughts as a springboard to deepen your spirituality. This means being ready to praise God for the offending thought or suggestion and using it as a stepping stone to draw closer to the Lord. If the proposal to thank God for an evil or impure thought offends you, then think it through with me carefully. Imagine you are walking down the street, thinking about nothing in particular, when an evil thought glides into your mind. What can you do? Some people advocate repressing the thought and pushing it back into the subconscious mind from whence it came. But repression is not the way, for repressed thoughts do not dissolve but continue to lurk in the dark corridors of the subconscious, waiting to express themselves in some other way. A better way is to take the offending thought and lift it to God in a moment of prayer and praise. Say, 'Thank you, Lord, for this wrong thought.' And why thank him? Because you are going to use it to draw closer to God. Before, you were walking down the street thinking about nothing in particular, but now you are going to use this thought to explore and experience the Saviour's love and power. You are going to think about him, meditate on him, and, if convenient, perhaps read a passage from the Scriptures. The thought, evil though it may be, is now being made into a stepping stone for closer contact with your Lord. It has become the means of drawing your attention to him. When the devil sees you taking the evil or impure thoughts he sends and using them as stepping stones to draw closer to God, he will soon give up, as he will see that he is in fact doing God's job for him.

So do not be afraid to meet temptation head on. See it as a challenge to deepen and not destroy what God has given you. If you face it in the spirit of complete dependence on the Lord, and with a determination to do his will, then you will come out of every wilderness experience as Jesus did—with the thrilling consciousness that power tested has become power triumphant.

# 11

# *Managing Your Finances*

'We feel a bit foolish coming to see you about a trivial thing like this, but it has been worrying us for some time, and we don't know anyone else we can ask.'

Bob and Hilda, a young married couple, had been Christians for about a year, but over the past few months they found themselves getting deeper and deeper into debt. They wondered at first whether they should stop tithing their income to their local church and use that money towards payment of their debt. Before taking this step, however, they decided to seek an outside opinion.

In our counselling session I posed this simple question.

'Let me ask you thing,' I said. 'Who is your biggest creditor?'

Hilda began to look through the invoices and bills she was holding in her hand, but Bob reached out and put his hand gently upon hers.

'Darling, don't you see what Selwyn is getting at . . . our biggest debt is not to men but to God.'

They came to see in that interview the importance of placing God at the top of their list of creditors, and making sure that his claim came first.

'Oh, just one other thing,' said Bob, as he was leaving. 'Do we tithe on our net income or gross income?'

'That's simple,' I replied. 'It depends which one you

want God to bless.'

Bob grinned as he steered Hilda through the door, then pausing for a moment looked back over his shoulder and said, 'the gross.'

Not all counselling problems are solved as simply as that of course, as sometimes one has to struggle with deep issues that need in-depth counselling stretching over several sessions. The Christian's relationship to money, however, is so clearly laid down in the Scriptures that there is no real difficulty in understanding how as Christians we should manage our finances.

## Temporal values

Material things have a way of mastering us. They deceive us into thinking that if we have *them* we have everything. A man made in the image of God must recognize that there are higher things than material possessions, or else he will become as metallic as the coin he seeks. We live in a materialistic age when there is a terrible attachment to *things*. Millions spend their existence on striving to get *things*. A new house, a new car, a better job, more shares . . . things, things, things.

Of course one should not *despise* material things, as they are given to us to enjoy, but the craving for possessions can get out of hand, and when this happens it elbows out everything else, so that people spend most of their lives striving to satisfy the craving for material possessions. They become covetous, grasping, greedy—and miserly too.

This desire for material things focuses in the pursuit of money. Money is equated with power, the power to command, to purchase, to persuade and to influence the lives of others. In every age there are multiplied thousands who discover that money cannot buy happiness, but unfortunately it is only those who posess it who know it. The rest of mankind press on in the belief that wealth and happiness go together.

A poor man in the company of a millionaire said, 'I am richer than you.'

'Don't be a fool,' the rich man replied. 'Look at my estate, my houses, my factories, You have none of these things. How can you possibly make a statement like that?'

'Well,' said the poor man 'it's quite simple. I have as much as I want . . . and you haven't.'

Everywhere in the Scripture God appears to associate our ability to handle material things with spiritual maturity. To some the challenge of responsibility in finances might be irksome, and there will be those who at this point will want to turn over a few pages and skip the important facts that are being discussed here.

The Scripture puts it succinctly when it says, 'The man who is faithful in the little things will be faithful in the big things, and the man who cheats in the little things will cheat in the big things too' (Luke 16:10 PHILLIPS).

Most Christians have been trained as money *earners,* not money spenders. Nevertheless all Christians have a personal obligation to spend money wisely, because they are stewards, not proprietors, of the finances God allows to pass through their hands. Below are several major principles which will help you relate to this whole problem of finances in the light of Christian stewardship and service.

## Transfer ownership to God

Recognize immediately that unless money is seen in relation to the wider perspective of eternity it can soon master you—and you do not need a million pounds sterling for that to happen. Money masters you when it convices you that it is the chief thing to work for, but Jesus said, 'A man's life consisteth not in the abundance of the things which he possesseth' (Luke 12:15), and 'where your treasure is, there will your heart be also' (Luke 12:34).

Sometime (as soon as possible after reading this chapter) lay all your possessions at the feet of Christ in a simple act of surrender, and let him know that you willingly and voluntarily transfer the ownership of all you have and are into his hands. Once you have done this you will know the peace and assurance that comes through the confidence that God can take care of everything that is put into his hands. The responsibility finally is no longer yours, but his! This act of transferring ownership is important—not because your money can be stolen—but because it can *steal.* It can steal control of your life.

## Remind yourself regularly of God's ownership

Tithing, that is giving one tenth of your income to God, is regarded by some as pertaining to the Old Testament teaching and having no application in modern times. They say that this system of giving was under the law—now we are living under grace.

In fact the very first mention of tithing in the Scriptures occurs long before the law was introduced, away back in Genesis 14:20—'And he gave him tithes of all.' This refers to the ancient patriarch Abraham who tithed his possessions to Melchizedek, a priest of the most high God. Later on, God reprimanded his people because of their failure to tithe, claiming that by so doing they were robbing him of his rightful dues. 'Will a man rob God? Yet ye have robbed me. But ye say, Wherein have we robbed thee? In tithes and offerings. Ye are cursed with a curse: for ye have robbed me, even this whole nation' (Malachi 3:8-9).

Sometimes I meet Christians who say they can't afford to tithe, but quite frankly this is dodging the issue. It is not so much that we can't afford to tithe, but that we can't afford *not to!* Thousands of Christians will tell how bountifully God pours out his blessing when his principles are obeyed.

'Bring ye all the tithes into the storehouse, that there may be meat in mine house, and prove me now herewith, saith the Lord of hosts, if I will not open you the windows of heaven, and pour you out a blessing, that there shall not be room enough to receive it' (Malachi 3:10).

## Educate yourself in basic matters

In the complex world of today, knowledge of basic financial matters is essential. Making ends meet is a critical problem in many Christian homes. Problems about insurance, buying a home, purchasing a car, borrowing money or buying on credit can quite easily be solved by a little patient and persistent study of the many excellent books on sale regarding these matters.

One of the major concerns to every Christian should be the use of credit. A recent investigation in the British Isles into the cause of bankruptcy indicated that in almost every case the reason was *overuse* of credit. Impatience to have the luxuries of life too fast brings thousands into financial bondage.

The more you examine the whole subject of finance and your responsibility towards it, the more you will be able to develop a spiritual sales resistance against the purchase of items you do not really need. Remember, high-pressure advertising pinches pounds from your purse, and in an age of powerful media communication a Christian should be on his guard that he does not squander the money God has committed to his care.

## A want or a need?

The following rules have helped many to evaluate the difference between a want and a need. Study them carefully and memorize them. They might be put to use sooner than you think!

1. Do I *need* this item or do I merely *want* it? (Philippians 4:19).
2. Do I have the money to pay for it?
3. Will this item make me more spiritually effective?
4. How much will it cost each time I use it?
5. Is there someone I can confer with before purchasing, who will give me a neutral opinion?
6. How much will this item depreciate in the future months and years?
7. Am I paying for features I do not really need?

## Develop spiritual sensitivity

The apostle Paul, writing to the Corinthians, said this: 'At present your plenty should supply their need, and then at some future date their plenty may supply your need' (2 Corinthians 8:14 PHILLIPS). One of the most important aspects of our relationships to other Christians is the need to develop sensitivity for those who are financially burdened. We have spoken elsewhere of the need to be sensitive to the spiritual needs of others, but we must be sensitive also to their financial needs.

It is God's desire that Christians should be fused together into a close spiritual fellowship, so that each becomes aware of the needs of the others. It was this that prompted the apostle in the above quotation to recommend to the Corinthian converts that they share from their prosperity, so that in future others may be able to give to them.

## Direction by withholding

There are times when God provides guidance for his children by deliberately withholding finances, thus preventing them from entering into situations in which they should not be involved. As I look back over my own life I thank God for the times when he withheld finances from me, or else I would have gone ahead with projects in which God was not interested. Here are a few suggestions you might like to consider on why God withholds finances from his children.

1. Because we don't really need it.
2. Because he wants to test our faith.
3. Because we may have previously misspent.
4. Because he is drawing our attention to unconfessed sin.
5. Because there is about to be a major change in our lives and he wants us to be free to move into a new area of responsibility.

## Giving and receiving

Throughout the whole of the Scriptures there are clear laws laid down by God to govern the success of our lives. These are non-optional, and we ignore them to our peril. Fulfilment (in a spiritual sense) lies in living in harmony with these laws, for obedience brings spiritual enrichment.

One of the most remarkable laws in the Bible is this. 'Give, and it shall be given unto you; good measure, pressed down, and shaken together, and running over, shall men give into your bosom. For with the same measure that ye mete withal it shall be measured to you again' (Luke 6:38). A similar verse, regarded by some as the ninth beautitude, can be seen in Acts 20:35—'remember the words of the Lord Jesus, how he said, It is more blessed to give than to receive.'

Someone might well raise the question, 'Once I have paid my tithes, isn't that enough?' The Bible not only talks of tithes but offerings as well. It's quite simple. You *pay* your tithes—that is an obligation. However your *give* your offerings, as that is something you do because you want to, not just because it is expected of you. In fact some teachers insist that you cannot possibly give an offering to the Lord until first you have paid your tithe.

A mistake many Christians make concerning giving is to say this. 'I will give to the Lord if he will give to me *first.*' This is contrary to that vital principle of giving and receiving which God wants each one of us to enjoy. God says *you* give *first.* Give . . . and it shall be given unto you, pressed down, shaken together and running over. In other words God says, 'You take this first step and I will take the next.'

Some years ago I sat in a missionary service when a special need was being presented regarding a missionary station across the seas. I felt as I prayed that God wanted me to give a certain amount to him in that offering, but the amount I felt impressed to give was so large that I hesitated. A struggle ensued but the Lord won and when the offering plate reached me I gave to the Lord exactly what he had asked. As soon as I dropped the amount in my offering on the plate I felt a great peace steal over my heart.

The next day a letter arrived containing a sum five times more than I had given in the offering the night before. It seemed God had put into action his own word that says, 'Before you call I will answer.'

This fixed law of the universe will work for *you* when you put it into action. But first you must give—*you* give—then God will give back in his characteristically abundant measure.

Giving to God enables God to give back to you!

# 12

# *Your Place in the Body*

'Me gifted? You gotta be kidding!' Carl, a young American over in this country on research work, came to me in between one of our seminar sessions seeking further enlightenment on a remark I had made concerning the fact that every Christian has a basic spiritual gift.

'If you knew how hopeless I am at everything,' he argued, 'I doubt whether you would say that.' I urged him to reserve his judgement as the point could not be further elucidated in the short span of a seminar break, and explained that the point would be dealt with in more detail at a later lecture.

He didn't appear to be too pleased with my suggestion, but at the end of the seminar Carl waited at the door until it was time for me to leave, then walked over to me and pumped my hand vigorously.

'Man,' he said, 'this is too much! I just discovered what is my basic spiritual gift . . . and I can't wait to go out and develop it. There it was all the time . . . staring me in the face . . . and I never knew it.' I knew exactly how he felt, for I remembered the excitement that flowed through my own heart when I discovered my own basic gift. The memory of that day lingers with me still.

## Every Christian has a basic gift

Are you a gifted person? Like Carl, you may be feeling inept or inadequate at this moment, but if you are a Christian the answer is yes! Whether you realize it or not, God has specially gifted you to fit into a special place in his plan, and designed you to fulfil a specific role in accomplishing his purpose for the world. Every Christian has a basic spiritual gift from God, and one way to add a thrilling new dimension to your Christian experience is to discover your basic spiritual gift and develop it.

'But what,' you ask, 'is a basic spiritual gift?' Just as in our natural birth there are abilities which become evident as we grow older, so at our *new birth* (conversion) God builds into our spirits at least one basic gift which enables us to minister effectively in the way God thinks best. Someone described it as 'the basic inward drive which God has given us, through which we can best manifest his love.'

It is not the same as a natural ability, such as an aptitude to play the piano—nor even a skill to write, speak or pass examinations. Confused? It's not surprising! Although the apostle Paul was clear in his epistles concerning the whole scope of spiritual gifts, the church has neglected to expound on this, to the detriment of its own spiritual welfare.

Here's a technical definition. A basic spiritual gift is a God-given ability bestowed upon a Christian at the time of his conversion enabling him to fulfil his function within the body of Christ. You may now ask 'What is the body of Christ?'

## The church—his body

The New Testament describes the church of Jesus Christ in four different ways, and by a curious coincidence they all begin with the letter 'b'. It is spoken of as a building, a bride, bread, and a body. When Jesus was here on earth *he* was God in human flesh. But after his return to heaven he sent back the Holy Spirit to form a new body so that his life could be perpetuated here on earth. That body consists of millions of believers all over the world, redeemed by his blood, and now part of that mystical union which stretches around the globe.

What is the church? Is it Gothic architecture, elegant masonry and stained glass windows? It is simply a stone edifice on which stands a steeple? No! The church is a farmer ploughing in the field, a housewife at the kitchen sink, a mechanic in the garage, a student in the classroom. Wherever there is a heart that knows the personal experience of Christ's saving power, there the church exists.

The church is the body of Christ. Not a denomination, an organization, or a special group, but all those who belong to him through personal faith in the Son of God. As members of that body we are also members one of another, and the purpose of our basic spiritual gift is not simply to express ourselves, but to *build up that body.* The apostle Paul put it thus, 'Now here is what I am trying to say: all of you together are the one body of Christ and each one of you is a separate and necessary part of it' (1 Corinthians 12:27 TLB).

## Joy through expression

One of the reasons for frustration among Christians arises from the fact that many believers have no positive understanding of their basic ministry within the body of Christ. Joy comes only when we discover our basic gift and *exercise* it in the way God has planned. This gift (or gifts) is bestowed in accordance with the wisdom of God, who in eternity foresaw our appearance in this world, measured our total capacities and built into us a drive that would best benefit his body.

As in the human body each part is designed to function in complete harmony and interdependence, so in the body of Christ he has positioned each one of us to perform a task of which we are definitely capable. Performing that task to the fullest degree is the calling of every Christian.

Many Christians are unaware of the rights and privileges we have as corporate members of the body of Christ. We saw in chapter one what God had purposed for us in *creation*, but now we must look at what he has planned for us in *redemption.* In fact our self-identity will not be complete until we see ourselves functioning effectively within his body.

It becomes clear when we read the New Testament that God does not expect any believer to live in isolation. In Matthew 18:19 Jesus said that if two Christians agree on earth concerning anything they ask, his Father in heaven will do it. He went on to say (verse 20), 'For where two or three gather together because they are mine, I will be right there among them' (TLB). And Paul said, 'Just as there are many parts in our bodies, so it is with Christ's body. We are all parts of it, and it takes every one of us to make it complete, for we each have different work to do. So we belong to each other, and each needs all the others' (Romans 12:4-5 TLB).

For the body to be in proper health, all of its members must function as they were designed to function. Each believer has different gifts and because of this has a particular role to play in the functioning of the body. If we are to reach our maximum potential we need to be part of a group of Christian believers who can teach each other, share with each other, confront each other, challenge each other, and pray for each other. Unfortunately too many Christians spend their time passing judgement on each other, condemning each other, and criticizing those who may not see things from *their* point of view.

## Our place in the body

Once we understand our real place and purpose in the body of Christ we will then see that we have a responsibility to minister to the needs of others. Often believers fail to recognize this, and instead of ministering to the needs of others with the special ability God has given them, they spend their time criticizing the actions of others, and fail to do anything constructive and positive towards bringing others to spiritual maturity.

As believers placed in that body, we need each other if we are to function in the way God designed, and we need to make a commitment to each other that will use every ability God has given us to first bring ourselves into Christ's likeness and then seek to bring others to that same maturity also.

One minister I know likes to tell a story of an eagle who built her nest in the tall trees but failed to make a bottom to the nest, so much so, that when the eggs were laid they fell straight through and smashed on the ground beneath. When asked why she did this, she replied (so the story goes): 'I enjoy laying the eggs but I don't want the responsibility of bringing up babies.'

Some Christians have an adverse effect on the body of Christ because they think everybody should be a mouth, a hand or a foot. They fail to see that as members of Christ's body we all have *different* gifts. They then set about encouraging others to be busy in the Lord's service and try to get them involved in every possible Christian activity. A great deal of damage has been done by well-meaning but misguided Christians who act in this way and cause confusion and frustration to others by their wrong advice.

## Maximum effectiveness with minimum weariness

In my teens several people persuaded me that I had the gifts of a pastor and ought to go to Bible school to train and study to that end. Instead of checking their evaluation against my own basic spiritual gift, I had little understanding of this subject so I followed their advice. The result was that although I had some success in the field of pastoral service, and churches grew and prospered under my ministry, inwardly I was frustrated and unhappy because my basic gifts did not include that of pastoral ministry and I was therefore achieving *minimum effectiveness* with *maximum weariness.*

When I discovered my basic gift and moved into the realm God really intended me to be, I then knew *maximum effectiveness* with *minimum weariness.* When a person begins to work in the way God has planned for him, then this service is not a grinding struggle but sheer delight.

When you see people in the church who are running around in what has been called 'the Christian rat race', trying to do so much and about to have a breakdown, you can be sure that person is not following the direction and leading of the Holy Spirit. They are probably letting other people dictate to them what they should be doing, and because they are afraid that someone might say they are not good Christians if they don't do it, they allow themselves to get talked into doing things that may not be in accordance with their spiritual gifts at all.

Someone might think you ought to be a preacher, and that you should go to Bible school, or that you ought to sing in the choir, or sit on a certain committee. You must learn to say, 'Let me pray about it first and find out whether this is in line with what the Lord has planned, and I will let you know.' Recognize that God has made you the way you are for a purpose. It is essential to your own success in Christian service that you become aware of your basic gifts.

We must share with others in such a way that we discover those gifts and use them. Don't model yourself on anyone else or copy the ministry of others, but find out what God has for you, then work with him.

How then do we go about discovering our basic spiritual gift? There are three sources of gifts seen in the New Testament, which come from the three different members of the Trinity. In Romans 12 we can read of the gifts which *God* gives; in 1 Corinthians 12 the gifts which the *Holy Spirit* gives; and in Ephesians 4 the gifts that *Christ* gives.

## Gifts we have

Let's look for a moment at the first stream of gifts outlined in Romans 12.

> Through the grace of God we have different gifts. If our gift is preaching, let us preach to the limit of our vision. If it is serving others let us concentrate on our service; if it is teaching let us give all we have to our teaching; and if our gift be the stimulating of the faith of others let us set ourselves to it. Let the man who is called to give, give freely; let the man who wields authority think of his responsibility; and let the man who feels sympathy for his fellows act cheerfully. [Romans 12:6-8 PHILLIPS.]

In this list there are seven basic gifts.

*Prophecy.* This word has a dual meaning in the New Testament. It means to 'pour out truth' or to 'show forth things that will happen'. It is used here in the sense of a God-given ability to present truth through the preaching of his word.

*Serving.* This means attending to the practical needs of others so that they can be freed for even more effective service.

*Teaching.* This means expounding truth by making clear the meaning of Scripture and involves careful detailed and accurate unfolding of the Bible's meaning.

*Stimulating.* An ability to encourage others towards spiritual growth by personal counselling and advice.

*Giving.* This carries the thought of an ability to organize one's personal affairs so as to invest financially in God's work. It also carries with it the ability to make wise and sound decisions regarding the right use of money.

*Ruling* (or wielding authority). An ability to preside or lead others by looking ahead and distinguishing major objectives and bringing others towards them.

*Sympathy.* An ability to sympathize with the misfortunes of others. The word carried the thought of empathy which involves deep emotional identification with those in distress.

To discover your basic gift, prayerfully go down the list and ask yourself, 'Which one of these gifts do I really identify with?' There will be one (perhaps more than one) which will become barbed as you read it, and will attach itself to your heart. Imagine that you are to be involved in the establishing of a church in your community and you are given the choice of one of the above gifts. Which one (after prayer and concentration before God) would you choose?

The one that leaps out at you and almost shouts 'pick me' is most probably your basic spiritual gift. As you identify with it your spirit will witness to what is happening and you will realize that you are discovering now what God placed in your life at conversion. Don't run over it quickly. Take your time, and pray it through. Check it time and time again until you know without any doubt where your basic gift (or gifts) lie.

Some of course will discover that there are two or even three gifts apparent in their lives, but it is wise to discover first the *one* that really stands out above all others. Joy will flow as you then seek to develop that gift in line with what God has given you to do and the ministry he has planned for you in his body.

## Gifts we receive

Your next step is to take the second stream of gifts as found in 1 Corinthians 12:8-10. There you will find that there are nine special gifts given by the Holy Spirit. Ponder these gifts, and consider carefully what Paul says in 1 Corinthians 12:31—'But covet earnestly the best gifts.' What are the best gifts Paul is referring to here? Quite simply the best gifts to *amplify and extend your basic gift* which by now you should have discovered.

You see, just as God has given you a basic gift which needs to be discovered and developed, the Holy Spirit is waiting to amplify that gift in accordance with his own supernatural enabling, and to equip you more effectively for that specific function God wants you to perform within his body. No one can achieve maximum effectiveness in the plan and purpose of God until they recognize the tremendous importance of the Holy Spirit's involvement in the Christian experience.

Just before he stepped out into his public ministry, Jesus came to the river Jordan where he was baptized by John the Baptist, and simultaneously received a supernatural empowerment from God, which equipped him for the special service he was about to perform. In that experience Jesus moved from the spiritual into the supernatural and received an anointing of power that enabled him to represent his Father in accordance with the plan that had been drawn up by them before the foundation of the world.

Although the Holy Spirit is involved in our conversion (John 3:5) we must allow ourselves to be open to his complete ministry in our lives, as he longs to make us like Christ in the sense that we have not only his purity, but his power too! Just before he departed to heaven Jesus promised his disciples that they would receive 'power from on high' when the Holy Spirit came upon them, and this of course took place in the Upper Room as recorded for us in the second chapter of Acts.

The experience that took place in the lives of those first disciples is available to you and me today. As you wait before God he will supply you with that same power he gave to his disciples close on two thousand years ago, and you too will experience the same supernatural enabling that both Christ and his disciples enjoyed.

## Gifts we become

We have looked at the gifts of God in Romans 12, and the gifts of the Spirit in 1 Corinthians 12. Let us look now at the final stream of gifts in Ephesians 4—'And he [Christ] gave some apostles . . . prophets . . . evangelists . . . pastors and teachers; for the perfecting of the saints, . . . for the edifying of the body of Christ' (Ephesians 4:11-12).

These five gifts of Christ are the people he selects for special work in his body and are put there by his own special and specific appointment. The first stream of gifts outlined in Romans 12 are the basic gifts which God builds into us at conversion. The second set of gifts as seen in 1 Corinthians 12 are the supernatural gifts he bestows as we enter the dimension of the Holy Spirit. The last stream of gifts are the people whom Christ himself selects for strategic ministry within his body.

If we begin to work out our spiritual goals by seeking to become evangelists, pastors or teachers, we will become extremely frustrated. For maximum effectiveness comes from first discovering our basic gift and then moving forward into a closer relationship with God's plan for our lives, as explained in previous paragraphs. When we discover and develop our basic gift (or gifts) in line with the Holy Spirit, then God will determine the final outcome of our ministry for him. If his plan for you is to make you an evangelist, a pastor, or a teacher, then it will become apparent as you move from one stage to the other. Discover your basic gift and God will determine your ultimate destiny. Concentrate on the first set of gifts; God will concentrate on the last.

It should be remembered that there is one special ingredient by which all gifts must be operated. It is love. This is the binding force between all believers, without which no gift can be properly exercised or expressed. With love flowing through my heart and with a clear understanding of my place in the plan of God, how can I ever want to change place with another? As I shape my progress on this principle I am no longer vulnerable to those who wish to impose their minds on what I should be doing for God. Once I am sure that *infinite* love and *infinite* wisdom are guiding my course, my whole being relaxes in the knowledge that God has planned the best for me, and co-operation with him will bring my life towards his highest ideal for me—to make me like his own beloved Son.

# God Wants You Whole

*The Way to Healing, Health and Wholeness*

**by Selwyn Hughes**

If God is always willing to heal, why do people remain ill—even when they have faith for healing?

How can we all live more healthy lives, day by day?

With openness and honesty, Selwyn Hughes faces squarely the issues of health and healing that concern every one of us. He examines the most common causes of ill health and the reasons we fail to receive God's healing grace. Here we see how our Creator has lovingly provided all we need for wholeness of living, if only we set ourselves to live in accordance with his will.

Above all, this book shows that even when healing eludes us and our condition is not remedied quickly, we can still rest secure in the knowledge that our heavenly Father is committed to our good—in spirit, mind, emotions, and body.

Also by Selwyn Hughes in Kingsway paperback:
*A friend in Need; How to Live the Christian Life; The Christian Counsellor's Pocket Guide; Everyday Reflections; A New Heart; Marriage as God Intended.*

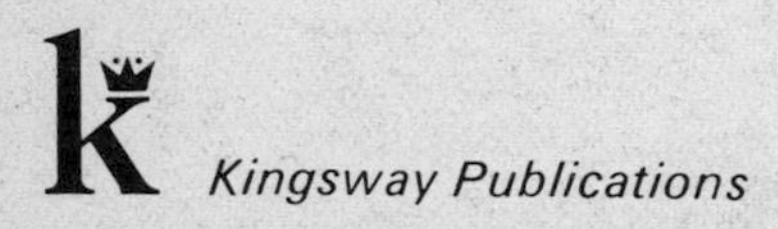

# A New Heart

*The promise of God to those who believe*

**by Selwyn Hughes**

Is a victorious Christian life possible? Can we know power and purity in our lives, and real faith?

Selwyn Hughes shows how God desires to win our hearts and so enable us to turn his promises into reality.

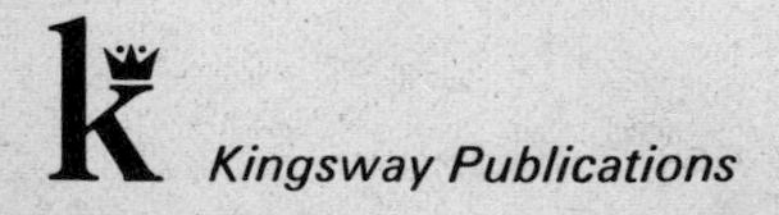

# The Christian Counsellor's Pocket Guide

**by Selwyn Hughes**

Have you ever been asked for help, or confronted with a challenge, only to find that your resources amount to little more than 'I think it says somewhere in the Bible . . .'?

Selwyn Hughes believes that no Christian need find himself in this position, and has therefore compiled this handbook of Bible references and practical advice after many years' experience in the counselling ministry.

*Section A* deals with the most common problems that trouble Christians;

*Section B* deals with objections raised by many unbelievers;

*Section C* confronts the most frequent intellectual excuses given as barriers to personal commitment.

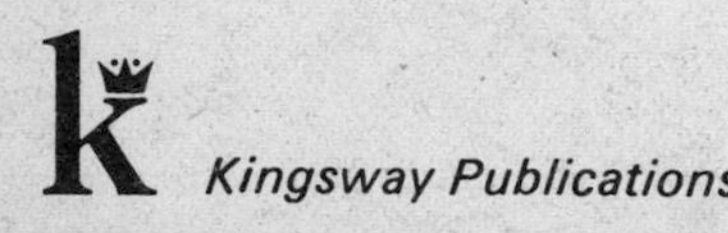

# Marriage As God Intended

## by Selwyn Hughes

*'We have never had an argument in the whole of our marriage,' said the husband.*
*'How did you accomplish that?' asked the counsellor.*
*'We just don't talk.'*

Communication is only one of the problem areas faced by married couples—there can be many other difficulties that cause us to fall short of God's perfect plan.

This book offers help—not only with specific problems, but for improving what is already good and healthy.

There are chapters on:
relationships with parents and in-laws
who's the head of the family?
sexual difficulties
the temptation to adultery
divorce and remarriage

Selwyn Hughes is highly respected as a leading marriage guidance counsellor. Here he draws on his many years' experience as both husband and counsellor, blending biblical principles with practical suggestions on how to let God keep your marriage at its best.